"Because *The Wonderful Wizard of Oz* is
speaks to its readers and viewers on b⌣
Dr. Morena shows the story to be what Baum could hardly have imagined
it becoming: a guidebook to our inner journey through the enchanted
land of Oz and home again."
   John Algeo, President of the Theosophical Society in America

"*The Wisdom of Oz* is making a valuable contribution not only to L. Frank
Baum's classic fairy tale, but also to the field of psychology."
   Kay Bradway, PhD, Founding Member of C. G. Jung Institute
   of San Francisco

"What makes *The Wisdom of Oz* particularly powerful is the clarity and
beauty of the style, and the honest and moving revelation throughout the
book of Gita Dorothy Morena's own struggles and progress on the Yellow
Brick Road."
   Maurice Friedman, PhD, author of *A Heart of Wisdom:
   Religion and Human Wholeness*

"*The Wisdom of Oz* invites one to explore the inner journey, invoking
questions about one's personal experience as well as cultural and mythic
themes that are unfolding in our time."
   Nicolee Miller-McMahon, Zen meditation teacher and Marriage,
   Family & Child Therapist.

"In this highly personal journey down the Yellow Brick Road, Dr. Gita
Morena reveals Oz, both the Great and Terrible in a remarkable new way.
Her great-granddad would have been proud."
   Michael Patrick Hearn, author of *The Annotated Wizard of Oz*

"If you are looking for a deeper, more informative view of America's one
perfect fairy tale…you can't do better than to start here."
   Independent Publisher

"Morena is the brilliant author of *The Wisdom of Oz*, an insightful book
that looks at *The Wizard of Oz* as a metaphor or personal growth, spiritual
transformation and inner healing."
   Metaphysical Review

"A marvelous look at yet another way Oz touches our lives, *The Wisdom of
Oz* is a fantastic addition to any Oz collection."
   Books of Wonder Publications, NYC

THE WISDOM OF OZ

THE WISDOM OF OZ
Reflections of a Jungian Sandplay Therapist

What we can learn from the real-life Dorothy,
Great Granddaughter of *The Wonderful
Wizard of Oz* author L. Frank Baum

GITA DOROTHY MORENA

This book is dedicated to Oz Lovers of all ages

TABLE OF CONTENTS

IN GRATITUDE

I want to thank all the people who have touched my heart, opened my eyes, held my hand, and loved me just as I am. May you be blessed with happiness and peace, surrounded with abundance, and showered with love and appreciation wherever you go.

My heart overflows with gratitude when I think of you: Greg and Brian, my esteemed teachers and beloved sons who keep me grounded and open my heart; my spiritual teachers, Osho who gives me the space to fly, Pujari who teaches me to stay focused and develop roots, and H. W. L. Poonja who focuses my attention towards who I am; my great grandfather, L. Frank Baum, who allowed Dorothy's adventure to flow through him; and my mother Ozma who introduced me to Oz and supported my journey home.

I thank all the people who have come to me as clients to forge through the unfamiliar territory of their inner world, and the students who have encouraged me to share the insights that have emerged along the way. I am most grateful for the support of my own sangha, the spiritual friends who gather with me regularly to meditate and expand in awareness. I particularly want to thank the people whose Sandplays were used to illustrate how the Oz characters speak for various concerns of the psyche. The names and stories of these contributors were changed completely so there identity can remain anonymous.

I thank the International Society for Sandplay Therapists; particularly Susan Macnofsky, Betty Jackson, Alexander Shaia, Barbara Miriello, Lee Ben Yehuda, Agnes Bayley, Kay Bradway, and others who suggested I write about Oz, gave valued suggestions for the emerging manuscript, and invited me to present this material to their students in workshops across the country.

I am most grateful to the many people who read and re-read the manuscript through its various stages of completion, and to the editors of the first edition who patiently assisted in the birthing process: Marlene Miriello, Debra Gingsberg, Clare Stebbing, and Andrea Glass. My mentor Maurice Friedman was an invaluable support, and Michael Hearn's editorial input as family historian was most helpful. Finally I am deeply grateful to North Atlantic Books for publishing thus second edition, and to Brooke Warner who has patiently and lovingly helped midwife it.

My dear friend and companion Bruce provided an island of sanity as the book materialized, my friends Sunny, Aman, Sid, Kara, Punit, Terri, and Sufi Baba were steadfast reminders that there is life beyond Oz, and Nicolee Miller-McMahon gently encouraged the emergence of my inner voice. I am deeply grateful to Chetna, who designed the original book and diligently persisted until the project was completed, and to Matt whose energy and enthusiasm brought *The Wisdom of Oz* to eager Oz lovers.

Without the love and support of this community, *The Wisdom of Oz* would have become a passing thought in the world of possibility. I thank all the spirits who have been present throughout this birthing process, and dance in celebration with the creative unfolding of live itself. May whatever merit comes from this project be for the benefit of all beings.

DEAR OZ LOVERS

I want to thank all of you who read the first edition of *The Wisdom of Oz* and responded with such enthusiasm and support. Your letters and personal sharing have touched me deeply and warmed my heart. Many of your comments have contributed to the revisions in this second edition.

In addition to restructuring the book for easier reading, now there is more information about Sandplay and how Oz is used for personal growth. I also discuss in greater detail the significance of Dorothy's travels back and forth between Oz and Kansas, and the struggles of her return to ordinary reality. The Return is an important and often overlooked phase of the hero's journey.

In my work as a psychotherapist and meditation leader, I have been privileged to participate in the healing of the psyche in an intimate and personal way. Often I marvel at how accurately the process of personal growth and awakening is exemplified by my great grandfather's fairy tale. It is a simple and masterful metaphor for the quest for inner peace, harmony, and happiness. Although Dorothy's adventures and the characters she meets in Oz are figments of L. Frank Baum's imagination, in many ways this fairy tale tells the story of all our lives. As a descendent of L. Frank Baum with the given name Dorothy, I identify with Baum's heroine in a most personal way. I was raised in what felt like Kansas, catapulted into unfamiliar territory that seemed like Oz, developed wisdom, compassion and courage from my life experiences and psychological understanding, and found my way back home by turning inwards on a spiritual path and connecting with the truth. At times I felt lost in an illusory land of make believe, but as later Oz books helped me understand, I needed to bridge my inner exploration with successful functioning in ordinary reality to become whole. If this concept interests you, read on. *The Wisdom of Oz* is about clarifying how Dorothy's experiences in Oz are really a template for psychological growth and spiritual awakening.

My birthday is August 1, the same day that *The Wonderful Wizard of Oz* was copyrighted nearly one hundred years ago. Because my name is Dorothy, when I first heard the story, I thought it was about me. My mother patiently explained that it was just a fantasy tale, but I was reluctant to accept her explanation. I must have been about six years old when she told me my great-grandfather, L. Frank Baum had written it. From that moment on, I knew in my heart that my life would somehow parallel Dorothy's marvelous adventures in Oz. As I grew into adolescence, I became intrigued with my family heritage and began to actively explore my relationship with Great Grandfather Baum.

L. Frank Baum, the Royal Historian of Oz, had four children. In 1914 his youngest son, Kenneth Gage Baum, married my grandmother Dorothy Hilda Duce. My mother was L. Frank's first granddaughter, and the first girl to be born into the family for two generations. He insisted that she be called Ozma. In his second Oz book, *The Marvelous Land of Oz*, Princess Ozma is discovered to be the true ruler of that extraordinary kingdom. As I learned about my family, I imagined my mother to be a princess just as L. Frank must have intended when he named her after the ruler of Oz. Unfortunately his health began to deteriorate about the time Ozma was born, and he died just before her third birthday.

The popularity of *The Wonderful Wizard of Oz* suggests that many of you identify with Dorothy and her adventures. Being lost and eager to return home is a common theme that underlies our existence. We talk about this in different ways according to our religious or philosophical upbringing, but a sense of separation and a yearning for some connection to a higher power is a universal feeling that pervades our experience. In the language of metaphor, *The*

Wonderful Wizard of Oz speaks to these issues and reminds us that the longing within our hearts can be satisfied. Ultimately we all want inner peace, happiness, and love. Dorothy is a powerful model from our own culture who shows us how to attain these heartfelt desires.

In everyone's life there are moments of awakening when our true nature is seen clearly and directly. These moments occur within the flow of our personal experiences and life stories. Like yellow bricks that build a road for the journey home, they provide opportunities to deepen our understanding and recognize who we really are. The surprise of Dorothy's adventure is that what she wanted was inside her all along. Although we travel great distances, ultimately there is no path and no outer destination to reach. Home is the acceptance of what already lies within.

The Wisdom of Oz was written to pique your curiosity and stimulate inner exploration by looking more carefully at your own travels along the Yellow Brick Road of life. It is only by planting and cultivating your own seeds of personal reflection that the flowers of wisdom will grow and multiply within you. If you are so inclined, I would be honored to hear your thoughts and insights about how the story has touched your life.

Although many of you are familiar with Dorothy's adventure as it appeared in the 1939 movie classic, I encourage you to read Baum's original story. There are a few significant differences that are interesting. As adults now, you may see how Dorothy's experiences reflect your own. Perhaps you feel caught up in a cyclone that is turning your life around and carrying you into territory that is strange and unfamiliar. Perhaps you feel the protection of the Good Witch of the North who has kissed your forehead to safeguard you against harm. Maybe you are encountering the wounded aspects of yourself in the form of the Scarecrow, the Tin Woodman, and the Cowardly Lion, or maybe your are facing insurmountable obstacles in an attempt to obtain your heart's desire. Some of you may be feeling the deep disappointment that Dorothy experienced when the Wizard did not fulfill her wishes, and others may be overwhelmed by the forces of the Wicked Witch who imprisoned

Dorothy in a castle of darkness and despair. Finally, some of you may have realized who you are and be returning home to share yourself with those you love.

If you are reading this book, you are most likely a person who is touched by the magic and seduction of fantasy. You know that fairy tales carry important lessons, and you are probably inclined to explore how these apply to your life. This is how bridges between the known and the unknown are created. Doorways open within us that allow our own natural wisdom to arise effortlessly. As you deepen with your personal relationship to a story, the power and inspiration of its message expands into your life.

As you examine Dorothy's adventure, I encourage you to remember the wonder of the child within who is enthralled with the magic of Oz. It is through honoring that inside place of enchantment and imagination that the joy of childhood is retained. May following this path of yellow bricks bring increased awareness into the daily experiences of your life, and may you discover the presence of your own magical slippers and awaken in the realization of your own inner home. Let light, love, and laughter surround you, and whatever merit comes from this book be for the benefit of all beings.

Your friend on the Yellow Brick Road,

Gita Dorothy

A NOTE FROM OZMA

Gita Dorothy Morena's mother
L. Frank Baum's granddaughter

In *The Wonderful Wizard of Oz* L. Frank Baum wrote about the adventures of Dorothy Gale traveling down the Yellow Brick Road towards home. A few years later the Shaggy Man stated in *The Road to Oz*, "Roads don't go anywhere. They stay in one place so folks can walk on them." Each one of us travels down a Yellow Brick Road meeting adversity and happiness as we go toward our individual destinies.

I was welcomed into the Baum family with open arms as the first granddaughter of L. Frank Baum. My grandfather insisted I be named Ozma, although my parents had chosen a different name. He also gave me a locket at my birth, with the name "Ozma" engraved on the back. I felt like Grandfather Baum had started me on my own personal journey down the Yellow Brick Road. Just as Glinda kissed Dorothy on the forehead for protection, I have always worn this locket to accompany me on my journey through life.

My father, Kenneth Gage Baum, was born in Aberdeen, South Dakota on March 24, 1891. He was the youngest son of L. Frank and Maud, and named in honor of his grandmother, Matilda Joslyn Gage. He was born on her birthday, and carried her spirit into our family. Some of the earliest memories of my father were his reading the Oz stories to me at bedtime. Feelings of warmth and love surrounded me, and I felt safe and protected even though there were moments in the stories that were frightening.

In my younger years the name Ozma was a burden to me. It was mispronounced, ridiculed as strange, and sometimes praised as pretty. My friends teased me by calling me "Cosmos." As a result I began calling myself Scraps, after the title character in *The Patchwork Girl of Oz*. She was fun, intelligent, and always getting into trouble. Somehow she reminded me of Grandmother Baum. As I grew older and my grandfather became more recognized, my name was not the burden it had been. I again called myself Ozma. I was proud of my grandfather and felt honored that he had named me.

I remember my visits to Ozcott, my grandparents home in Hollywood, California. I spent many happy times there with my grandmother, and always considered it my second home. Maud was a tall and commanding figure, both intelligent and strong willed. She was a great influence in my life. I loved to read and just look at the books in her library at the end of the living room. I would curl up in one of the large chairs and be transported into strange lands. Sometimes my cousin Robert also visited, and together we spent hours with the books, especially enjoying Gustave Doré's scary pictures in Edgar Allen Poe's set of horror stories.

Through the influence of Grandmother Baum I felt the support of my great-grandmother, Matilda Joslyn Gage, who seemed to be guiding my reading and encouraging my interest in medicine. Matilda's father was a physician who tutored her at home from his extensive library that emphasized the sciences. He instilled in her a belief in the rights of the individuals. Not only did she give speeches along with Susan B. Anthony and Elizabeth Cady Stanton, but wrote three volumes of the *History of Women's Suffrage*. Her strong conviction about women's rights passed through her children and grandchildren, and influenced the women of our family. Because of her attitudes, it never occurred to me that I could not accomplish and obtain any goal I chose.

My journey after college began in medicine as an R. N. The obstacles thrown my way were mainly losses. The death of my mother on the day I was married to Kenneth A. Mantele, M.D. and my father's death a few years later were severe traumas in my life. As a pediatric nurse working on the oncology unit at Children's Hospital in Los Angeles, I encountered many children dying of Leukemia. After 37 years of marriage my husband died of lung cancer, which was the most devastating and trying time of my life. While going through my own grief, I continued to work at a hospice counseling children who had a significant death in their family. The black shadow of the grim reaper seemed to confront me at all turns on my journey.

As a mother, I have had to stand by and watch Gita-Dorothy fight her own battles in life. She is now coming into her own, and it is beautiful to see her express herself in writing. As she continues on her path down the Yellow Brick Road may her words bring pleasure to all her readers. May the spirit of her great grandfather be with her and guide her home, just as it guided Dorothy in *The Wonderful Wizard of Oz*. As Glinda kissed Dorothy on the forehead for protection, so my love accompanies my own Dorothy on her journey with destiny.

Ozma Baum Mantele
June 1997

Ozma and Dorothy Gita (1996)

THE EVOLUTION OF OZ

L. Frank Baum (c. 1915)

CHAPTER ONE
THE ORIGINS OF OZ

You are welcome, most noble Sorceress, to the land of the Munchkins.
We are so grateful to you for having killed the Wicked Witch of the
East, and for setting our people free from bondage.
L. Frank Baum, *The Wonderful Wizard of Oz*, Chapter II

Imagine yourself at the turn of the century. Light appears miraculously with the flick of a switch, carriages run freely without horses, and friends living miles apart talk to each other through wire
cables. Americans are dreaming about ways to improve their lives,
women are fighting for the right to vote, and a plethora of innovative products are flooding the marketplace to lighten the chores of
daily living. It is a wonderful, exciting, and deeply disorienting time.

In the midst of this creative vortex, a children's story captivates
the hearts of children and adults alike. A lost little girl from the
heartland of America bravely faces adversity and eventually finds
her way home. Her name is Dorothy, and her adventure in Oz is
one of the most beloved stories of the twentieth century.

The Wonderful Wizard of Oz made its debut into American literature in 1900, when the fabric of society was rapidly changing
and the pace of daily living was increasing. Manufacturers were
multiplying, women enriched the work force, and America's western frontier was no longer an unexplored wilderness. Dorothy's
arrival in the Land of Oz marked the entry of Americans in a new
reality. In the symbolic language of fairy tale, *The Wonderful Wizard
of Oz* addressed an underlying uneasiness that was just beginning
to permeate the culture at the turn of the century. Through its

imagery, people could see how to navigate successfully through a variety of disturbing situations in territory both new and unfamiliar. Americans embraced Baum's fairy tale wholeheartedly, perhaps in an attempt to find their way through the pervasive changes surrounding them.

High-powered technology and scientific feats of wonder are common occurrences in the world today. Although designed to ease the burdens of life, these modern inventions have stimulated flurries of activity that generate waves of confusion and alienation. In an attempt to keep up with the increasing pace of daily living, people are moving faster and faster, as if caught on the rim of rapidly spinning wheels. Without a sanctuary for relaxation though, they are unable to sustain a sense of inner tranquility and understanding. The central axis of their spinning wheels has been forgotten, and the order, stability, and direction that originates there has been lost.

Although L. Frank was unaware how his story would impact future generations, he anticipated and responded to people's internal struggles and needs with intuitive sensitivity. In an interview with a family friend he described how *The Wonderful Wizard of Oz* came into existence.

> It was pure inspiration. It came to me right out of the blue. I think that sometimes the Great Author had a message to get across and He was to use the instrument at hand. I happened to be that medium and I believe the magic key was given to me to open the doors to sympathy and understanding, joy, peace, and happiness. (Potter, "The Man Who Invented Oz," 1939)

Thirty-nine years after *The Wonderful Wizard of Oz* was published, images of Dorothy's adventure blazed before the American public in bold Technicolor. "Toto, I've a feeling we're not in Kansas anymore," Dorothy exclaims in the popular MGM move. Her words were spoken to a nation poised on the brink of a second world war. They reflect the disturbance of a country whose industrial, political, and technological developments shattered the familiar fabric of everyday life and paved the way towards destructive global conflicts. The story of this orphaned child must have paralleled the unspoken sentiments of family and friends who feared loosing their soldiers on the foreign battle-fields of World War II.

Almost twenty years later, *The Wonderful Wizard of Oz* appeared on family television sets to a generation of children who rocked the nation with their revolutionary ideals. The flower children of the sixties seemed to follow in Dorothy's footsteps as they left the security of their family homes and attempted to create loving communities that embraced diversity and fostered peace and harmony.

The Oz story has remained relevant and true to each generation since its conception. With synchronistic perfection, the centennial anniversary of its publication coincided with the dawn of a new millennium. What began as a tale to entertain children has become one of the many instruments of collective awakening. Just as the little girl who traveled in Oz reassured the fears and concerns of previous generations, this timeless story continues to address the internal struggles that plague mankind. It speaks universally to lighten the heart, soothe the soul, and awaken the memory that happiness lies within.

THE BIRTHING OF OZ

Storytellers are masters at weaving tapestries of imaginative events into entertaining tales of wonder and enchantment. L. Frank Baum was one of the best. Children flocked around him, captivated with his adventures into magical fairylands. It was a tradition in the Baum household to share stories before bed, and often neighborhood children would appear to participate in this treasured ritual. Baum's flights into fantasy became such a popular event that a constable stopped by the household around nine o'clock every evening to accompany the young visitors home. The fact that the Oz story developed from a dialogue with children may help explain its magnetism and continued popularity.

It is difficult to trace the origins of most fairy tales. They arise from the telling and re-telling of people's most favored stories. With L. Frank Baum though, it is possible to uncover some of the thoughts and associations that inspired this beloved tale. In 1898, the year Baum was working on the Oz manuscript, his niece Dorothy, died in infancy. He and his wife Maud loved the little girl, and the family speculates that he named his heroine after her. The image of the Emerald City resembles the turrets and towers of the World's Columbian Exposition in Chicago in 1893. A few years before *The Wonderful Wizard of Oz* was published, Baum had moved his family to Chicago hoping the exposition would increase his opportunities for work. In an interview about the origins of the name "Oz," Baum describes how he weaves images from his environment into the rich tapestry of his fantasy worlds.

> I was thinking and wondering about a title for my story, and I had settled on "Wizard" as part of it. My gaze was caught by the gilt letters on the three drawers of the cabinet. The first was A-G; the next drawer was labeled H-N; and on the last were the letters O-Z, and Oz it at once became. (Baum, interview *in St. Louis Republic*, 1903)

Millions of copies of *The Wonderful Wizard of Oz* have been sold since it was first published in 1900. It had been printed in more than a dozen foreign languages, and American audiences have been entertained with film and stage productions since the turn of the 20th century. In 1902 the musical comedy, *The Wizard of Oz*, began a tour that lasted nearly a decade and included two successful runs on Broadway. In 1910 Dorothy's adventures were portrayed in a silent move production, and since then stories of Oz have been recounted in numerous silent and sound movies, radio shows, musical comedies, operettas, puppet shows, audio recordings, and other stage productions. "We're off the see the Wizard," "We're not in

Kansas anymore," Follow the Yellow Brick Road," I'm melting," and "There's no place like home," are common phrases to the American public, and words such as "Munchkins," Cowardly Lion," Poppy Fields," Toto," and "Oz," have entered the American vocabulary. References to the story appear almost daily in books, newspapers, magazines, television, advertisements, and commercials. There is everything from an electronic Wizard of Oz game for Nintendo users, to Ruby Red Shortbread for Oz lovers with a sweet tooth. Images of the Land of Oz appear on T-shirts, mugs, posters, tennis socks, computer mouse pads, clocks, stamps, canisters, suspenders, and watches. There are Wizard of Oz dolls, pins, costumes, music boxes, figurines, post cards, greeting cards, stuffed toys, games, jewelry, jewelry boxes, and everything else imaginable.

Baum completed fourteen Oz stories, and Ruth Plumly Thompson followed with nineteen more after he died. Other Oz stories continue to be published. Dick Martin, Eric Shanower, Jack Snow, Rachel Cosgrove, John R. Neill, Eloise Jarvis McGraw, Lauren McGraw Wagner, and L. Franks' great-grandson Roger Baum, have carried on the Oz series. In Texas, a fifth grade teacher was so excited about creating adventures in Oz that for many years his students wrote, illustrated, and published Oz stories as a classroom project under the name "The Wiz Kids of Oz." *The Wiz* is a popular stage show and movie that adapts the story to the black inner-city ghetto, and *Zardoz* is a science fiction movie that refers to the power of the *Wonderful Wizard of Oz* and its influence in an imaginary future. As the story is told and retold, it expands and develops, stimulating the imagination and inspiring the creativity of those who encounter it.

In 1957, Oz enthusiasts gathered together to create The International Wizard of Oz Club. Their magazine, *The Baum Bugle*, is filled with Oz information and research. Every year members gather around the country for Oz conventions. Groups representing the Munchkins, Winkies, and Quadlings meet in the eastern, western, and southern United States respectively.

The growing use of Oz imagery in the American culture points to the strength and power of L. Frank's metaphoric language. He was able to express values and concerns with images that people continue to appreciate and find useful. Through the simple characters of a scarecrow, a tin man, and a lion, deeper attributes of wisdom, compassion, and courage are exposed. Through the diversity of Oz the value of a person's uniqueness is revealed. The relationships of the characters emphasize the importance of preserving integrity while living harmoniously. As the dawn of this new age begins to brighten consciousness, Oz lovers continue to expose and admire the gems of ancient wisdom embedded in this meaningful fairy tale. With Dorothy's adventures appearing in movie houses and television sets across the country, *The Wonderful Wizard of Oz* has became a main thoroughfare bridging the magical world of storytelling and the wondrous world of modern cinematography.

RECOVERY OF THE FEMININE

My great-great-grandmother, Matilda Joslyn Gage, inspired the creation of Dorothy by encouraging her son-in-law to publish his most requested children's stories. Although Matilda died before *The Wonderful Wizard of Oz* was written, Dorothy's story would have resonated with her ideals and visions for women.

After raising four children, Matilda Gage worked closely with Elizabeth Cady Stanton and Susan B. Anthony on the *History of Women Suffrage*. She later explored the historical origins of women's oppression in her major work, *Women, Church and State: The Original Expose of Male Collaboration Against the Female Sex*. She wrote with conviction, "Freedom for women underlies all the great questions of the age. They must no longer be the scapegoat of humanity upon whose devoted heads the sins of all people are made to rest." (Gage, *Women, Church and State*, 1893). From childhood to her death in 1898, Matilda fought valiantly for freedom on all fronts. Her influence as an active suffragist and dedicated freedom fighter played an important role in the development of the heroine who would come to be known worldwide as Dorothy.

Women suffragists at the 1888 meeting of the International Council of Women in Washington, D.C. Matilda Gage is seated second from the right, next to Elizabeth Cady Stanton. (1988)

Baum was an early feminist supporter who was unafraid to acknowledge the value of women in the marketplace. In his editorials for *The Aberdeen Saturday Pioneer*, he commented regularly on the activities of the suffragists and spoke directly about the strength, intelligence and wisdom of American women. He encouraged their participation as leaders in politics, stating without reservation: "If our politics are to be masculine forever, I despair of the republic." (Baum, *The Aberdeen Saturday Pioneer*, 1890).

Baum's fairy tale of a strong and adventurous heroine appeared at a time when women were finding their voices after centuries of persecution and oppression. Throughout the Middle Ages women were burned at the stake as witches for their activities as healers. Their intuitive powers were greatly feared and they were forced underground in order to survive. With the domination of the patriarchy, refusal to comply with male authority was not tolerated. The ways of the feminine were seen as threatening, and women were judged as inherently wicked and sinful. Even in men, the more feminine traits of sensitivity and tenderness were scorned and ridiculed.

It is crucial now for the energy of the feminine to be retrieved and integrated back into the culture. Without nurturing and support, people become disconnected and self-destructive. Today both men and women are struggling to rescue what has been suppressed and devalued by society. The Oz fairy tale speaks clearly to people who fight for these values.

Traditionally male heroes are depicted as action oriented with tough, aggressive, and self-confident attitudes. Women are considered heroic only if they emulate these masculine characteristics. Somehow a little farm girl manages to win the respect and praise of men and women alike. Although she is strong willed and determined, she is also quite vulnerable and kindhearted. She embodies the feminine characteristics of intuition and sensitivity while following the call to adventure. True to the ways of women, Dorothy steadfastly maintains her connection with family and friends, and avoids the aggressive use of violence by expressing her feelings when she is disturbed. She shows us how to pursue the heroic path in a courageous and feminine manner, by resolving difficulties without resistance or blame, and communicating openly with others. In the last hundred years, women have become more visible as significant forces in the culture. Just like Dorothy, they have encountered numerous obstacles and difficulties in their struggle for freedom and recognition. *The Wonderful Wizard of Oz* reflects their fight for freedom from the patriarchy and encourages the expression of their inner power.

In the symbolic language of this fairy tale, Dorothy leaves a harsh, unaccepting, male dominated farmhouse to travel to a lush, magical, maternal land of blooming abundance. She dives directly into the lost energy of the feminine, confronting its dark forces and following its call into the unknown. When Glenda tells Dorothy her Silver Slippers will carry her home, she returns to Kansas empowered as a women and inundated with the magic of Oz. Aunt Em's loving embrace welcomes her into a new farmhouse. The healing energy of the feminine is readily recognized and absorbed by a culture hungry for transformation.

THE PATH OF A HEROINE

Dorothy represents the archetypal orphan embarking on a heroic journey. Her departure from the familiar farmlands of Kansas, into the unknown Land of Oz and back again, embraces the Call to Adventure, Initiation, and Return that characterizes all heroic journeys. Heroes are often catapulted into their adventures by unforeseen calamities or natural catastrophes. Although the Call comes unexpectedly, the hero or heroine must willingly accept their participation for the journey to continue. The required tasks must be completed alone, but willingly accepting the challenge elicits the support of supernatural help and protection. When the swirling cyclone deposits Dorothy in Oz, a good witch appears to offer assistance and Munchkins gather to celebrate and send her on her way.

Dorothy then enters a stage of Initiation where she is challenged with adversity and difficulties, and must successfully fulfill the Wizard's command to retrieve the Wicked Witch's broomstick. She becomes trapped in the castle of the Wicked Witch, and like all heroes enters a dark period of isolation and gestation. Although the situation appears hopeless, Dorothy is actually enclosed in a womb-like chrysalis that becomes a sanctuary for transformation.

In the final phase of a journey, the hero stands before the Queen Goddess of the World, who represents the totality of all that is known. Through their interaction, the hero becomes aware of the importance of the journey and all that has been learned. After the Wizard fails her, Dorothy travels to Glinda, the Good Witch of the South, who acts as an archetypal goddess. By following Glinda's guidance to close her eyes, turn her attention inwards, and clarify her intention to return home, Dorothy experiences her inner resources and claims mastery over her life. Through the Scarecrow, the Tin Woodman, and the Cowardly Lion, she internalizes and manifests her own wisdom, compassion, and courage. Like all heroines, when Dorothy realizes what she desires is already within her, she begins the stage of Return, where she arrives home to share her newfound wisdom.

Like all archetypal heroes, Dorothy leaves the comforts of the known to venture into the darkness of the unknown. She returns from that yonder zone with wisdom that can only be attained through experience. By navigating between worlds that are familiar and worlds that are unknown, heroes unite what was once considered separate. They acquire a sense of wholeness, completion, and healing that psychologically mends the fragmented psyche. Traveling between worlds once thought to be divided opens the possibility that the treasures of home may be discovered within an undivided self.

The Wonderful Wizard of Oz touches the hearts of many people who are traveling this hero's path like Dorothy. The road is not always smooth and easy however. In some places the bricks are bright, solid, and evenly spaced, but in other places they are chipped, worn, and overgrown with moss and weeds. When the road goes into the deepest areas of darkness, there is no path at all. Like the yellow bricks Dorothy follows in Oz, awareness and understanding appear in the psyche as flashes of insight. They weave threads of experience into meaningful patterns and reveal the direction of our destination. In order to proceed successfully, these yellow bricks must be discovered and honored, so the way home can be easily recognized and followed.

Although heroic stories such as *The Wonderful Wizard of Oz* depict the journey of one person, in truth they describe the basic challenges of everyone's psychological and spiritual development. Like a kaleidoscope of moving colors, the story of Oz delights the imagination, playfully portrays the essence of a hero's adventure, and artfully provides a platform for the observation of our own journey. The name Dorothy comes from the Greek work Dorothea, which means "gift of God." Baum brought us the gift of Dorothy's story and we have woven its magic into our culture. Join me now as we discover for ourselves the pathway home.

CHAPTER TWO
THE MAN WHO CREATED OZ

I am also a child, for since I can remember my eyes have always grown big at tales of the marvelous, and my heart is still accustomed to go pit-a-pat when reading of impossible adventures.
L. Frank Baum, *A New Wonderland*

Christmas was fast approaching and L. Frank Baum responded reluctantly to his wife's request to secure an advance for his most recently published book *The Wonderful Wizard of Oz*. The children's story had become a desirable item for Christmas shoppers, and Maud was eager to make this Christmas a memorable event in the Baum household. The Family had been struggling for years, and she was hopeful the winds of fortune would shift favorably in their direction. Frank returned home with a folded check that he had not seen. The unexpected windfall of almost $2500 so shocked them that Maud inadvertently burned the shirt she was ironing. The magic of Oz was working wondrous effects in the Baum household, and the Christmas of 1900 opened the doors for a literary love affair with Oz that has continued throughout the century.

As L. Frank Baum's great-granddaughter, I often wonder about this man and the circumstances that inspired his writing. What kind of person gives birth to a fairy tale that touches the heart and inspires the imagination of so many? He obviously had a unique way of seeing the world, and was able to communicate this in a most entertaining and captivating way. In a world that prizes conformity and following trends, Baum stands out as a beacon of light, creativity, and individuality.

Maud Gage Baum, L. Frank's wife (1880)

Although he edited a newspaper in South Dakota and a trade journal on window trimming in Chicago, Baum wrote primarily for children. His thoughts, feelings, and beliefs are woven into his fairy tales, and the nature of his character can only be discerned through family stories, letters, and reminiscences. Like scattered puzzle pieces, the perceptions of family and friends blend to form an illusive image of this man who gave birth to a legend.

FRANK'S EARLY YEARS

Lyman Frank Baum was born on May 15, 1856 in Chittenango, a small town in central New York. He was the seventh of nine children born to Benjamin and Cynthia Baum. Two of Frank's siblings died before he was born and one died a few days after his birth. Because of these losses and Frank's fragile health, his parents were very protective of him. He spent hours alone, wandering freely over their country estate or absorbed in the English novels and European fairy tales in his father's library. *Pilgrim's Progress* was one of his favorites, along with the stories of Grimm and Andersen.

Frank's father's family was German. They were among the thousands of Palatinate people who fled to England, and later Holland, to escape religious persecution in the 1600's. In 1748 Frank's great-grandfather established himself in America as a farmer. Frank's mother, Cynthia Stanton Baum, was of Scots-Irish descent. The Stantons were among the first settlers in America, arriving in 1635 and becoming successful farmers in Connecticut and later central New York.

The Stantons did not support their daughter Cynthia's marriage to Benjamin Baum, a young and financially insecure barrel maker. He was a diligent worker though, and when oil was discovered in Pennsylvania, he gained their respect by expanding his enterprise and becoming quite wealthy. He moved with his growing family to a large farm surrounded with rolling green hills which they named Rose Lawn. It was here that their son Frank first saw scarecrows, and perhaps planted the creative seeds for the lush green countryside of Oz.

As was the custom for wealthy families, Frank and his siblings were educated at home with a private tutor. When he was 12, Frank was sent to Peekskill Military Academy, but the rigid and disciplined atmosphere was disagreeable to him. Two years later he returned to Rose Lawn, and resumed his independent study.

One day while traveling with his father on a business trip, Frank became fascinated with the small printing presses that were popular at the time. His father purchased one for his birthday, and he and his younger brother Harry began a neighborhood newspaper. They called it the *Rose Lawn Home Journal*, which included their own short stories, poems, word games, and neighborhood news. A few local businesses advertised in it and the boys did simple printing jobs for the neighbors. Later Frank edited a small monthly journal, *The Empire*, which contained postage stamp news, literature, and poetry. He became an avid stamp collector and before he left home, self-published a small pamphlet called *Baum's Complete Stamp Dealer's Directory*.

During his late teens Frank raised Hamburg chickens, a small, colorful, purebred fancy fowl. He formed a partnership with his brother Harry and soon won countless prizes at fairs and exhibitions. His first book, *The Book of the Hamburgs: A Brief Treatise upon the Mating, Rearing and Management of the Different Varieties of Hamburgs*, is about this youthful hobby. Hamburg chickens lack incubating instincts and are dependent on an attentive breeder to survive. The caring sensitivity and patient nurturing that Frank later demonstrated with his four sons must have been evident early on.

NAVIGATING THE RIVER OF LIFE

As Frank entered his young adult years, he became interested in acting and joined a local theater group. At first his family did not approve, but later his father built an opera house in Richburg, New York that Frank managed for a few months before it burned to the ground. In 1881, Frank produced *The Maid of Arran*, a play based on William Black's popular Scottish novel, *A Princess of Thule*. In addition to writing the script, he composed the songs, directed the play, and acted in the lead role. The production was well received, and Frank's troupe toured successfully.

That same year Frank attended a Christmas party at the request of his sister, Harriet Neal, who was eager to introduce him to a young family friend. Although Frank was reluctant to attend, his participation that evening was a significant turning point in his life. Frank's cousin insisted he would love Miss Maud Gage, and when introduced he flamboyantly proclaimed, "Consider yourself loved, Miss Gage." This was the beginning of a grand and tender love affair that continued throughout both their lives.

Maud was the youngest daughter of the woman suffragist Matilda Joslyn Gage. Matilda was a strong-willed woman who expected her daughter to follow her into the battle for woman's rights. The day Frank proposed to Maud, he overheard her talking to her mother and later shared his observations.

> I heard Mrs. Gage say: "I won't have my daughter be a darned fool and marry an actor." Maud snapped back: "All right, mother, if you feel that way about it, good-bye. "What do you mean, good bye?" Mrs. Gage demanded. "Well," Maud replied, "you just, told me I would be a darned fool to marry an actor, and you wouldn't have a daughter of yours do that. I'm going to marry Frank, so naturally you don't want a darned fool around the house." (Baum & MacFall, *To Please a Child*, 1961)

Maud's mother gave in, and the young couple married with her blessing on November 9, 1882. They toured with *The Maid of Arran* until Maud became pregnant, and then they established a home in Syracuse, New York. Eager to care for his new family, Frank left the theater, joined his father's oil business, and marketed Baum's Castorine, an axle lubricant designed to keep carriage wheels running smoothly. Perhaps this was a premonition of the importance of the Tin Woodman's oil can, and the necessity of keeping him well lubricated to be functional.

Although good fortune seemed to have surrounded Frank since childhood, in the mid 1880's a series of misfortunes plagued him. Frank's father was injured in a buggy accident from which he never fully recovered, and without his astute leadership the family suffered. After his father's death, Frank was eager to expand the family business. He met with resistance though, and in 1888 he and Maud moved with their two sons to explore greener pastures in South Dakota. Frank was excited about establishing his own business in the booming frontier town, and Maud was delighted to rejoin her family who had settled there.

TRAVELING WEST

Baum's Bazaar, a variety store of quality goods, opened its doors in Aberdeen, South Dakota shortly after the Baum's arrival. Frank was optimistic about its success, but soon the town was plagued with severe droughts and economic depression. Frank was forced to close the store just a year and a half later.

Frank then became owner and editor of one of Aberdeen's weekly newspapers. He printed the local and national news from syndicated boilerplates and proudly dubbed the paper *The Aberdeen Saturday Pioneer.* His development of a humorous column called "Our Landlady" brought chuckles of delight from his readers, and his editorials provoked residents to examine current issues from a fresh perspective. His thinking was clear and forthright, and at times he was bold and impulsive in sharing his opinions and ideas.

Many images appeared in Baum's children's stories that originated while in Aberdeen. The vast plains of Kansas are reminiscent of the flatlands of North Dakota where his sister-in-law owned an isolated farm. Frank was intrigued with cyclones that transported entire houses for miles; and when severe droughts threatened local farmers, he suggested feeding the cows wood shavings and having them wear green spectacles to disguise it as grass.

Although Frank did not attend church regularly, he explored Theosophy while in Aberdeen and supported their teachings about the universality of God and the pervading influence of spirits. He later joined the Theosophical Society and incorporated his spiritual beliefs into daily living. The depth of his insights is reveled in a letter written in 1918 to his oldest son.

> I have lived long enough to learn that in life nothing adverse lasts very long. And it is true that as the years pass, and we look back on something which, at that time, seemed unbelievably discouraging and unfair, we come to realize that, after all, God was at all times on our side. The eventual outcome was, we discover, by far the best solution for us, and what then we thought should have been to our best advantage, would in reality have been quite detrimental. (Baum & MacFall, *To Please a Child*, 1961)

In spite of financial difficulties Baum maintained a generous, light-hearted, positive attitude, and was generally well liked by the townspeople. He made friends easily and his presence in local theater groups and community gatherings was valued. Frank's two younger sons were born in Aberdeen, and he was dedicated to creating a warm and loving family for them. Although accused of spoiling the boys by his wife, he was a devoted and encouraging father who promoted men's participation in child rearing.

THE ROYAL HISTORIAN OF OZ

Financial difficulties continued for the Baum's and the family finally moved to Chicago in 1891. Frank found work as a journalist for *The Evening Post*, but when the paper refused to pay what he expected, he began selling china and glassware. His creative window displays brought attention and sales, and he eventually founded *The Show*

Window, a periodical for window trimmers. Later his son Harry described one of Baum's displays that resembled the character of the Tin Woodman.

> He wanted to create something eye-catching, so he made a torso out of a wash boiler, bolted stovepipe arms and legs to it, and used the underside of a saucepan for the face. He topped it with a funnel hat, and what would become the inspiration for the Tin Woodman was born. (Haas, "A Little Bit of 'Oz' in Northern Indiana," 1965)

When Frank was home he enjoyed weaving fanciful stories for children. Maud and her mother encouraged him to publish them, and in 1897 his first children's book Mother Goose in Prose appeared. Frank was forty-one years old and wrote nostalgically to his sister.

> When I was young I longed to write a great novel that should win me fame. Now that I am getting old my first book is written to amuse children. For, aside from my evident inability to do anything 'great,' I have learned to regard fame as a will-o-wisp which, when caught, is not worth the possession; but to please a child is a sweet and lovely thing that warms one's heart, and brings its own reward. I hope my book will succeed in that way and that the children will like it. (Baum, *Mother Goose in Prose,* 1897)

The publication of *Mother Goose in Prose* encouraged Frank to devote more time to writing for children. He collaborated with artist W. W. Denslow on *Father Goose, His Book,* a book of whimsical verse that was a best seller in 1899. He loved playing with words, and expressed his bold and satirical humor through poetry and puns. Following this publication, Baum was inspired to write down one of the children's most requested stories about Dorothy. He describes this moment precisely.

I was witting in the hall, telling the kids a story and suddenly this one moved right in and took possession. I shooed the children away and grabbed a piece of paper that was lying there on the rack and began to write. It really seemed to write itself. Then I couldn't find any regular paper, so I took anything at all, even a bunch of old envelopes. (Hearn, *Annotated Wizard of Oz*, 1973)

Later Baum again collaborated with Denslow to produce the colorful and creative images in the first volume of Dorothy's adventure. Because no publishing house would risk the expense of these full-color pictures, Denslow and Baum financed the first printing of *The Wonderful Wizard of Oz* themselves. Its success exceeded everyone's expectations, and children around the country demanded more stories about the magical land. At first he had no intention of continuing the story, but Baum promised one little girl to write more about Oz when he had received one thousand requests. Much to his amazement the letters multiplied, and in 1904 he honored his promise by issuing his second Oz book *The Marvelous Land of Oz*. In it, he develops the theme of women rising in power, and describes how the Land of Oz comes to be ruled by Princess Ozma.

During the next 15 years Baum wrote prolifically. In addition to fourteen Oz books, he authored five other stories, over thirty single volumes, more than forty plays, and a number of poems, articles, songs, musical scores, and short stories. He employed a variety of pen names, so his material would not appear to flood the marketplace. At one point a successful publisher was interested in negotiating a contract with Edith van Dyne, the pen name under which Baum wrote the successful *Aunt Jane's Nieces* series. Baum's agent chose a female representative for the meeting and although he was present, Baum was forced to remain silent to protect his anonymity. Everything went quite well, however Baum declined their offer for additional publications so that his identity could remain hidden.

Baum wrote his manuscripts in longhand and edited them on a typewriter before sending them to his publisher. He liked to work outdoors, and often set up a desk in the garden or on the porch. (1899)

Although the success of his writing allowed the family to live more comfortably, Baum spent money freely and lived without saving or planning. From 1906-1908, he enthusiastically promoted the Oz stories with *Fairylogue and Radio Plays*. In these, he narrated his stories while slides or silent film provided a backdrop for actors and musicians to perform. Because of extensive production costs, he was forced to declare bankruptcy in 1911, and relinquished royalties from the Oz books to cover his debts. It was not until after his death that Maud once again received remuneration from the popular series.

After many winters writing at the Coronado Hotel in San Diego, Frank and Maud built a home in Hollywood which they called Ozcott. Frank planted a garden there, and when he was not writing he tended flowers. He particularly enjoyed the dahlias and chrysanthemums, which blossomed under his loving care and earned him many awards and trophies. Frank was fascinated with the booming movie industry of Hollywood, and founded the Oz Film Manufacturing Company. A number of silent Oz films emerged before Universal Studios absorbed the company in 1916.

During the last years of his life, Frank suffered from gall bladder attacks and tic douloureux, a painful condition that produced unexpected facial spasms. In 1918 his gall bladder was removed, but he never fully recovered. Frank was bedridden during the last year of his life.

Before he lapsed into unconsciousness on May 5, 1919, Frank reassured Maud that he always loved her and she would be well cared for. Frank was bridging the final barrier between this world and the world beyond death, just as his stories bridged the Desert of Shifting Sands that separates Oz from ordinary reality. Like Dorothy traveling over this vast sandy desert to return home, eventually each of us passes through the door of death and across the boundaries of existence to return home to our place of origin. With his passing, Frank reminds us that Oz is more than a fairy tale. It is a metaphor for the final journey we all must take.

A touching eulogy by a friend appeared in a Los Angeles magazine shortly after frank's death.

We love best those who make us see the most in ourselves. The man to talk to is the one who stimulates thought in ourselves. Now and then we meet a man who is like a fine mirror in which we see all the unexpressed beauty and nobility of our own natures. We think the man is wonderful because we ourselves are never so wonderful as when with him. His presence elevates us to those pure heights whereon we should always be walking, hand in hand with our ideals. Such a man was L. Frank Baum, beloved of all who knew him for the power of thought and the goodness that he aroused in all he met. Frank was the comrade of gladness; he walked with joy, and on his lips were the praises of life. Into his maturity he brought the sweet flowers of his childhood and they neither withered nor lost their fragrance. His influence upon America was beyond measure for he spoke to the children of the land. To give wings to the imagination and flame to thought is an endowment that is godly. In this power L. Frank Baum was wonderful, and his life was a benediction to the world. He taught children to dream and he brought them within the glow of his own enthusiasm of thought. He was not a churchman, but he lived the religion of delight and he belonged to the world of fine things. He had no creed, but he possessed abundant spirituality; with him the spiritual was a living experience. His soul was too full of light to harbor one thing that was small or mean, and his love was so great that it put white arms about humanity. (*Mercury Magazine*, 1919)

Chapter Three
Oz on Film

The little girl gave a cry of amazement and looked about her, her eyes growing bigger and bigger at the wonderful sights she saw.
L. Frank Baum, *The Wonderful Wizard of Oz*, Chapter II.

"Follow the Yellow Brick Road" is a familiar refrain that brings to mind images of cyclones, witches, sparkling emeralds and a little girl dressed in blue gingham. With MGM's creative use of Technicolor in the 1939 movie, the popularity of Oz skyrocketed. Audiences were filled with wonder and delight when Dorothy left the monochrome world of Kansas and opened the door to the rainbow richness of Oz. This innovative and enchanting production of the movie established *The Wonderful Wizard of Oz* as one of the most popular fairy tales in the world.

It was Judy Garland's first major movie production that brought Dorothy to life in 1939. Judy won an Academy Award as Best Child Actress that year, and was catapulted into a legendary career in entertainment. In addition, Ray Bolger, Jack Haley, Burt Lahr, Frank Morgan, and Margaret Hamilton immortalized the Scarecrow, the Tin Woodman, the Cowardly Lion, the Wizard, and the Wicked Witch. Harold Arlen and E. Y. Harburg's "Over the Rainbow" won an Oscar for Best Song, and musical director Herbert Stothert received an award for Best Original Score. The unusual special effects used in the Oz classic are still studied today in college film courses, and imitated by many move studios. When it is shown in large screen movie houses, it continues to draw capacity crowds.

In 1956, *The Wizard of Oz* first appeared on nation-wide television. Its yearly broadcast became a holiday tradition in many American households. With availability on videotape, it can be viewed easily throughout the year. For some it brings memories of childhood, and plays a part in consoling and comforting people. Recently a woman who was struggling with a difficult divorce shared with me how soothing and reassuring it was to see Dorothy and her companions follow the Yellow Brick Road and discover once again the way home. Later a friend shared that when she became homesick while studying in India, she gathered a group of American friends together to watch the beloved story.

Since *The Wonderful Wizard of Oz* first appeared in 1900 it has been lovingly and enthusiastically received. In 1925, Chadwick Pictures produced a silent movie version featuring the comics Larry Semon and Oliver Hardy, and in 1939 MGM established the story permanently in people's mind and hearts with their well-known rendition of the story. Recently the American Film Institute declared *The Wizard of Oz* the sixth greatest American movie produced during the first 100 years of American filmmaking.

Today people are more familiar with Hollywood's dramatization of Oz than the original book. Sadly, Baum's fairy tale is often left to collect dust on forgotten bookshelves. I encourage you to take a look at the original story rather than let the move industry promote their own rendition.

OZ IN TECHNICOLOR

Numerous people were involved in creating MGM's movie script. Characters and subplots were added and deleted as the story bounced from writer to writer, through various revisions. Noel Langley carried the primary responsibility for adapting Baum's book to film, introducing the concept of Oz as Dorothy's dream, and determining the direction of the final script. The revision by Florence Ryerson and Edgar Allean Woolf eliminated many of Langley's subplots and additions, and clarified the main objective of the film as Dorothy's struggle to return home. Writers were hired and fired throughout 1938 before Langley, Ryerson, and Woolf were given final screen credits.

Both the movie and the book are sympathetic towards Dorothy and the conditions she endures at her aunt and uncle's farmhouse. When she rescues Toto from danger though, Dorothy's love and courageous dedication shine as brightly in the movie as they do in Baum's original story. The general theme of being lost, encountering difficulties, and finding the way back home is preserved in the movie, and the overall spirit and message of the story remains intact. The Scarecrow, the Tin Woodman, and the Cowardly Lion are devoted to Dorothy, and in her presence they develop their abilities to function successfully. The Wicked Witch is destroyed in the movie just as she is in the book, and the Wizard is exposed as a humbug who is unable to keep his promises. Dorothy's image is maintained as a brave and beloved heroine who is devoted to her family and determined to overcome all obstacles that impede her return home.

One of the most treasured additions to the Oz story comes from Judy Garland's soulful plea for happiness in the song "Over the Rainbow." After a long storm the appearance of a colorful rainbow caresses the heart with a smile of delight. This vibrant arc of color taps into a childlike sense of wonder that creates a magical bridge into the realm of fantasy and imagination. Through its enchantment we are inspired to search for what lies beyond. A rainbow holds a promise of heartfelt happiness and dreamlike treasure. It is no surprise that it has become intricately linked with the Land of Oz.

LESSONS HOLLYWOOD LOST

Judy Garland was sixteen years old when she assumed the role of the Oz heroine. Although she was dressed as a child, her growing body could not be disguised, and a young adolescent replaced Dorothy's childlike character. Her adventures were portrayed as the visions of a dreaming child who had been knocked unconscious during a cyclone. When she regained consciousness, patronizing family and friends trivialized her experiences as figments of her imagination. The traditional image of women as weak and frivolous had found its way into the Oz film. In 1939, Dorothy stood for all women who were trapped by the unconscious attitudes and projections of the patriarchy. Although the movie portrays her adventures in Oz with vivid color and enthusiasm, its conclusion is disappointing and in sharp contrast to Baum's original story.

The integrity of Dorothy's traveling companions is well maintained in the 1939 movie, although their appearance as farmhands in Kansas is a bit misleading. The Scarecrow, the Tin Woodman, and the Cowardly Lion are pictured as images from Dorothy's dream world. Their protective and loving qualities are emphasized with their dedication to Dorothy, but they are no longer seen as reflections of her inner experience. The MGM movie links Dorothy's life in Kansas and Oz by perpetuating the illusion that the magical land is a figment of her imagination. The concept of Oz as a symbolic embodiment of Dorothy's psyche is lost, and the psychological implications of her journey as a development of her internal inadequacies is avoided. In blazing Technicolor Dorothy continues to be disempowered when her male friends receive what they want and she is left with empty promises.

Just as the three farmhands appear in Dorothy's Oz adventure, so do Mrs. Gulch and Professor Marvel find their way into her dreamlike experience. In the movie, Mrs. Gulch, a mean spirited Kansas woman, tries to take Toto away from Dorothy. Her pursuit continues in Oz as the threatening Wicked Witch of the West. Professor Marvel, the traveling gypsy from Kansas, becomes the "great and powerful Wizard of Oz." He hides behind a façade of magical marvels, and points Dorothy towards home both in Kansas and in the Land of Oz.

In the original story, Baum describes many harrowing difficulties that are not included in the movie script. While traveling to the Emerald City, Dorothy and her companions leap over deep crevasses, escape wild Kalidahs, cross a raging river, and rescue themselves from the hypnotic seduction of a fragrant Poppyfield. Later they overcome the harrowing assaults of the Wicked Witch of the West as they advance into her territory. The Scarecrow eliminates a destructive flock of crows, the Tin Woodman stops a devouring pack of wolves, and together they defeat a swarm of killer bees. Later, as the four travelers attempt to visit Glinda in the South, they are impeded by the Forest of Fighting Trees, a giant spider, a land of breakable figurine-like people, and an attack from the indestructible and hard-headed Hammerheads. It is in overcoming these hardships that Dorothy and her companions develop their inner resources. Their difficulties represent the struggles that come with any major undertaking, and their success is what inspires hope and encouragement for the journey home.

The Wizard of Oz movie eliminates nearly all the challenges of Dorothy's journey. Although the Scarecrow uses his intelligence to outwit the fighting trees, this is the only time the travelers must depend on their inner resources. There are no ravines to cross or fierce animals to escape. When sleep overcomes them while crossing the Poppyfield, Glinda magically creates a snowstorm to break the spell of the Wicked Witch. When the Wizard flies off in his balloon without Dorothy, Glinda appears quickly to help. By dismissing the challenges of Oz, the MGM production undermines Dorothy's character and minimalizes her development of wisdom and strength.

According to MGM, Dorothy's adventures in Oz revolve around avoiding the Wicked Witch of the West. Caught between good and evil, Dorothy acts as an innocent victim incapable of rescuing herself. When she arrives in Oz, Glinda the Good Witch of the North protects her with a kiss just before the Wicked Witch of the West threatens her with the words "I'll get you, my pretty." Glinda and the Wicked Witch are established enemies, and Dorothy lands in the middle of their battlefield.

Although Dorothy does melt the Wicked Witch of the West in both the book and the film, her climactic confrontation with the evil witch is compromised in the MGM extravaganza. In the film Dorothy throws a pail of water to protect her friend the Scarecrow, who catches fire when the Wicked Witch tosses a match on him. Because the Witch is standing in the background, the water inadvertently splatters and melts her. Dorothy's confrontation is no more than a fortuitous accident, and her image of being a victim of circumstance is maintained. In sharp contrast to the movie, Baum describes Dorothy as outraged when the Wicked Witch tries to take the Silver Slippers by tripping her with an invisible metal bar. Dorothy angrily hurls a pail of water, accessing a deep power and range that lay dormant within her. Perhaps the writers of the move script were afraid to unleash the potent feminine energy that had been locked within Dorothy's indomitable spirit.

When the travelers return to the Emerald City Dorothy is devastated that the Wizard is a humbug and therefore unable to fulfill her request. He plays an important role in recognizing the wisdom, love, and courage of her companions, but in the presence of Dorothy his true nature as a pretender is revealed. Although Dorothy admonishes him for being a bad man, he replies with honesty and humility, "Oh no, my dear, I'm really a very good man; but I'm a very bad Wizard, I must admit."

In Baum's book, the Wizard speaks wisely to the Scarecrow, the Tin Woodman, and the Cowardly Lion about the traits they desire, and bestows on each of them a symbol that resembles their requests. To the Scarecrow he gives sharp pins and needles for brains, to the Tin Woodman he offers a silk heart for love, and to the Cowardly Lion he prepares a potion for courage. His acknowledgement and validation of their respective traits allows them to see clearly who they are.

In the movie the Wizard's gifts are represented as accolades to acknowledge achievement: a diploma for intelligence, a testimonial for kindness, and a medal for courage. This small change points to a misunderstanding that often arises when striving for particular goals. Recognition of success is frequently mistaken as a substitute for what is real. Accruing the praise of another individual does not necessarily indicate the presence of particular qualities. As Baum intimates through the Wizard's comments to Dorothy and her friends, wisdom, compassion, and courage come when a person uses their inner resources to respond to life's challenges.

Although the Wizard fulfills his promise to Dorothy's companions, he is unable to satisfy her. In both the movie and the book, Dorothy must suffer the disillusionment of shattered expectations before discovering the way home. Although she believes in the Wizard and eagerly anticipates riding home in his balloon, Toto prevents her from following the well-intentioned humbug. Just as the hot air balloon begins to rise, the little dog disappears into the crowd. Dorothy chases after him and misses her flight home. Had she left with the Wizard, Dorothy's story would have dissolved into the familiar headlines of "Damsel in distress rescued by knight in shining armor," and the internal wisdom of the feminine would have disappeared. Fortunately the guidance of Toto prevents her from falling into the clutches of false promises and beliefs. Dorothy remains in Oz to realize her own inner power.

At this point in the story there is a substantial difference between Baum's original story and the Hollywood rendition. At the end of the movie, Glinda appears miraculously in a clear crystal bubble and shows Dorothy how to use her magical slippers. In the original story though, Dorothy embarks on another long and difficult journey to meet with Glinda, the Good Witch of the South. It is here that Dorothy learns about the power of her Silver Slippers. Once again, Baum's story emphasizes the development of internal awareness that comes by engaging with life directly, rather than being magically rescued by an outside force. In the book, the Good Witch of the North greets Dorothy when she arrives in Oz; and Glinda, the Good Witch of the South, guides her home. These powerful women mark Dorothy's entrance and exit from the extraordinary kingdom, but they do not directly interfere with the lessons she learns there.

Many people are surprised to discover that the Ruby Red Slippers are silver in Baum's story. Apparently the producers of the film felt the visual impact of these powerful shoes would be lost if they retained their original color. In the MGM film Dorothy's red shoes appear boldly on the road of yellow bricks, highlighting their importance with the change in color.

Although there are many significant differences between the book and the movie, the 1939 adaptation of Baum's fairy tale indelibly imprinted the Land of Oz into the American psyche. Red Slippers, Flying Monkeys, Witches, Scarecrows, Tin Woodmen, and talking animals have captivated audiences around the world, and elaborate movie sets, songs, and dances continue to seduce viewers into a magical land of enchanting entertainment.

A TEMPLATE FOR HEALING

CHAPTER FOUR
THE ADVENTURE BEGINS

You must go to the City of Emeralds. Perhaps Oz will help you.
L. Frank Baum, *The Wonderful Wizard of Oz*, Chapter II

Disasters catapult people into experiences beyond ordinary reality. Although there are many ways to initiate a heroic journey, the call to adventure usually comes unexpectedly. Death, divorce, and natural catastrophes force us to examine our deepest beliefs about the world. We must willingly cooperate though, to retrieve the insights contained within their chaotic turmoil.

Because our experiences are constantly changing, we must continually adapt to new situations. Resisting life's flow only creates pain and suffering. When we try to control external circumstances, we prevent ourselves from recovering the treasures of wisdom and understanding that are embedded in life's spontaneous events. Concepts of the past, anticipations of the future, and attachments to how we think things should be must dissolve so we can respond to what is happening in the present moment. As we identify past conditioning and limiting beliefs, our perceptions of reality clarify and we are able to act with more freedom and less confusion. When Dorothy lands in Oz she does not believe in witches, and is startled to hear animals talking and to see scarecrows walking about. Her willingness to surrender outdated beliefs and preconceived ideas allows her to embrace her role as heroine and accept these strange events without hesitation.

Dorothy remains surprisingly calm when the cyclone pulls her away from all that is familiar and carries her into the strange country of Oz. Although it is a frightening event, this catastrophe allows for the emergence of something new in her life. Dorothy falls asleep while the storm rages around her, and awakens refreshed and responsive to her unusual circumstances. Perhaps her relaxed willingness to move into unknown territory is an example of how to surrender and adjust when forces operate outside our control.

Although storms often create a pathway of destruction, they are respected expressions of creative energy and acts of divine power. In primitive cultures, the eye of a cyclone is honored as a passageway to other dimensions of reality. Dorothy's sleep suggests the Land of Oz is an altered state that expresses the unconscious material of her psyche. Perhaps her experience in Oz can be seen as a visual manifestation of her inner world, and like a dream represents hidden associations that reside there. Not to be dismissed as an imaginary dream state though, the images in Oz are more precisely expressions of her inner reality.

TOTO TAKES THE LEAD

Dorothy's adventure begins in a Kansas farmhouse when she attempts to rescue her beloved Toto from a threatening storm. In Latin, "totus" means whole, complete, or entire. Perhaps the presence of her canine friend is what gives Dorothy a sense of wholeness. He is quick to defend his mistress and eager to accompany her into Oz.

Animals function naturally without reasoning, and in the language of symbology represent our intuitive or instinctual energy. They are companions of goddesses and healers, friends of witches, faithful allies of mankind, and messengers between physical and supernatural worlds. Because of their all-seeing vigilance and acute sense of smell, dogs are valued by hunters and esteemed as guardians and protectors. They stand as sacred sentinels before passageways into the afterworld, and accompany individuals as they travel into the nether regions.

In the process of psychological and physical healing, a person often descends into dark, shadowy, death-like states where they confront and conquer unknown forces. This is a difficult period of internal reorganization that is experienced as empty, forsaken, solitary, and depressing. It is followed by an ascent into health and rebirth when the life force re-ignites to stimulate a new sense of wonder and delight. How reassuring it is to have the presence of a protective companion who senses danger, and is unafraid to navigate into the frightening and far-reaching corners of this unknown territory.

I am reminded of a brilliant young man who was working successfully in a large law firm as a well-respected attorney when he came to see me. JR had chosen this profession to please his father, and found himself feeling restricted and unhappy with his choice. He wanted to examine and eliminate the reasons for his unhappiness. As we worked together, he realized how important his father's approval was to him, and how he rarely felt that his actions pleased him. This is a pattern that had developed when his parents divorced during his early childhood. He had decided as a young child that if he were good enough, his father would return to the family. This belief still dominated his thinking as an adult, although it was buried in the nether regions of his unconscious.

After a year of verbal therapy where JR addressed these difficult feelings about his father, he decided to take life into his own hands and leave the law firm. He lived off his savings for a while, battling feelings of depression and confusion about who he was and what he wanted to do. Without the security of a professional identity, he retreated from family and friends. Like Dorothy, his only solace through this difficult period was his little dog who brought him joy and made him laugh. Although quite uncomfortable, JR patiently accepted this time of incubation, and when sparks of creativity urged him to towards pottery, he followed the call to immerse himself in an exploration of ceramic art. He was an adept student, and blossomed with the development of his creativity. Eventually he began to work in retail stores using his gifts to design merchandise displays. As he became more visible in the work world, his employers frequently consulted him for legal advice. He finally returned to the law profession but continued to develop his artistic skills. Through his willingness to let go of everything and discover who he was, JR found a harmonious and satisfying way to use his abilities and education. Oftentimes the journey home requires a sacrifice of everything that is familiar, to uncover the true gems of our identity and create a satisfying place in life

Wholeness comes as the psyche integrates newly revealed aspects of the unconscious. This includes the healing that happens when a person accepts their inner intuitive wisdom, and opens to the confusing tensions of the inner world. For many people, dogs represent a relationship to what is irrational and instinctive. Pet owners honor their four legged friends for the wisdom and companionship they provide, and are often able to enter unknown territories when accompanied by their faithful friend. Certainly for JR, the presence of his canine companion provided the comfort necessary to stay on his path of self-discovery.

I remember the outrage and grief I felt as a young child when our family dog died and my parents refused to honor their promise to let me have another. I sank into the recesses of my inner world and began to consciously experience the uncharted territory of anger, loss, and betrayal. At first I felt abandoned and victimized by the situation, but as these feelings released, things shifted within me. The underlying sorrow of loosing a dear friend led to an awareness that relationships do not end with death. I began to experience and trust a world of invisible forces and intuitive wisdom. A sense of inner guidance and protection emerged, and I moved with increasing delight into mysterious regions of the psyche. It was as if the dog I had known as a child marked the way into the previously unexplored territory of my inner world, and instilled within me an awareness of my own instinctual energy. Although my early companion did not remain in physical form, true to the ways of dog-spirits, he became one of my guides into psychic realms.

Now I have a little Maltese dog that accompanies me wherever I go. He is friendly and lovable, and has been a great companion through the deaths of my fiancé and mother. His unconditional love and enthusiastic delight with whatever is happening, is a constant reminder of the simplicity of life, and his instinctual sensitivity to danger is a blessing. He has become an integral part of my healing practice, for myself as well as for my students and clients.

Although Dorothy rests calmly while the arms of a raging storm carry her house through the skies, Toto, in sharp contrast, races wildly around the moving room. It is difficult to imagine being relaxed in the midst of a full-blown cyclone. Perhaps Toto's instinctual energy embodies the uncomfortable feelings that Dorothy is unable to express at this time. His black color represents what is unmanifest, irrational, and not easily perceived, and his behavior reveals the intensity of powerful forces that hide in unexplored regions of the unconscious.

Without Toto, Dorothy would never have discovered the way home. Her rush to save him from the storm initiate her journey to Oz, and later her chasing him for the balloon ride home protects her from becoming caught forever in the Wizard's illusion of power. It is Toto who discovers the humbug hiding behind a screen, and Toto who prevents Dorothy from flying off in his repaired balloon. External forces like good and bad witches and wizards cannot interfere with Dorothy. She must find the means within for saving herself. The impetus and guidance for her success in Oz is sparked by her devotion to Toto, and her strong instinctive responses to life's circumstances.

IDENTIFYING WITH DOROTHY

Dorothy Gale touches the heart of anyone who has suffered great loss and endured hardship. Those who identify with her relate to the catastrophic events of her early childhood and the bleakness of her life in Kansas.

As an innocent child, Dorothy readily bonds with the Scarecrow, the Tin Woodman, and the Cowardly Lion when she arrives in the Land of Oz. She relies on her new friends whenever she encounters difficulties, and with the naïveté of a child, believes the Wizard will readily grant each of their wishes. Dorothy becomes discouraged when she is told to kill the Wicked Witch of the West to obtain her request. If she fails, she will remain a child in Oz. If she succeeds, she will activate internal powers and step out of childhood forever. She reaches a climactic point of initiation when she faces the Wizard and hears his request. Her willingness to accept his challenge is what begins her development as a woman.

When L. Frank created Dorothy, he endowed her with the archetypal energies of adventure, adaptability, openness, and determination. Dorothy comes from the heartland of America and represents the quintessential characteristic of all Americans. She epitomizes the spirit of early American pioneers who eagerly absorbed new experiences and courageously faced life-threatening hardships. Her lack of resistance to strange phenomena and her willingness to face adversity without complaint makes it possible for her to enjoy her experiences and quickly adapt to unfamiliar situations. Her indomitable spirit is unmatched in many traditional European fairy tales where children are generally portrayed as vulnerable and powerless. When the frontier territories within America were closing, Dorothy blazed a trail into the interior regions of the psyche. Her presence marks the beginning of an era of psychological exploration that has continued throughout the century.

For many adults Dorothy's journey awakens memories and feelings that have been hidden since childhood. The neglected child that is buried within the psyche dances in delight as Dorothy escapes the harsh surroundings of Kansas and lands in a colorful country filled with adventure and friendship. Dorothy is a reassuring reminder that the child within is loveable, honorable, and acceptable, and that there are worlds other than Kansas waiting to be explored.

I am reminded of a 43-year-old woman who used images from Oz to express her inner discovery of an innocent, lovable child who had been locked behind bars of self-hate and negativity. Estelle was raised in a dysfunctional and emotionally abusive family where she was identified as a "problem child." As a rebellious teenager, she entered a dark world of drugs and promiscuity, leaving home to find her own way in the world. In her early twenties she returned to school, and began a journey of self-discovery that has led her into a profession as a healer. Although she was able to break free of her family to establish a healthy relationship and successful career, the scars of her childhood haunted her. She was filled with feelings of self-doubt and insecurity, and unable to see her own strength, wisdom, or beauty. She lived her life in fear and self-hatred, and was guarded and anxious in her interactions with others.

Estelle was fascinated with Sandplay, excited about unlocking her creativity, and eager to address the struggles of her inner world. After many months of verbal and Sandplay therapy, she created a scene in the sand where the Scarecrow, the Tin Woodman, and the Cowardly Lion approached a burning candle enclosed on four sides by small screens (Sand Scene 4-1). She described the trepidation she felt with the screened off area in the center of the tray saying "yesterday I felt the fear to be big and empty, like these screens, and when I look inside of the emptiness there's a candle, the light. I never would have though that. And the Oz characters are here - the Tin Woodman, for the heart, and the Lion for courage. I almost left out the Scarecrow because he's for thinking, and I feel I have enough of that. But then I realized he would be for wisdom, and that made sense." We talked about the wonder of this moment, and the realization that was growing inside of her, that she was good and filled with light.

Sand Scene 4-1

In her next session (Sand Scene 4-2), Estelle placed four lighted candles on the edges of the tray, removed the screens, and set a baby in the center on the sand. Glinda, Krishna, angels, elephants, and an Aztec goddess surrounded the infant who sat before a piece of birthday cake. Tears came as she recognized the birth of her self, and together we celebrated by singing "Happy Birthday."

Sand Scene 4-2

During the weeks that followed, Estelle described how the Scarecrow, the Tin Woodman, and the Cowardly Lion represented the understanding, love and courage that had grown in her. She was profoundly affected by the appearance of the baby in her sand scene, and her life spiraled upwards as she softened with newfound love and respect for the vulnerable child that lived within her. She had found an important part of herself, and was now ready to enter and explore the world.

The inner child can be described as the embodiment of our intuitive function and a personal expression of our divine nature. It is the part of us that feels orphaned on this planet, and like Dorothy yearns to return home to that state of oneness from which we originated. If we listen to the voice of this child, we will be led along the Yellow Brick Road and shown the way to satisfy our profound longing for happiness. Dorothy encourages us to recognize and follow the voice of this child. In a way she is the child within each of us. Trusting and opening this inner child connects us with our own intuitive wisdom, and allows us to explore new and stimulating situations without hesitation. Fortunately we have the template of Dorothy's story to show us what can happen when we break free of established patterns and move into a direct experience of life's mysteries

BEGIN AT THE BEGINNING

Dorothy's instinctive desire to protect Toto begins her adventure in Oz. By saving her beloved dog, Dorothy shows us the value of preserving and including the intuitive function in our activities. The importance of natural instincts is further emphasized when Dorothy opens the door and is enthusiastically welcomed by the Munchkins. The Little People become the symbols of Dorothy's instinctual energy that is now available to fuel the most important journey of her life. Dorothy's arrival in the Land of Oz liberates the Munchkins from the Wicked Witch of the East, and they dance in celebration of their newfound freedom.

Although young and inexperienced, as is often true for newcomers, Dorothy is blessed with divine protection and guidance. When catapulted into tumultuous experiences, unexpected support and serendipitous assistance often come our way. It is as though surrendering to life's catastrophes allows the blessings of divine intervention to manifest. Because her house killed the Wicked Witch, Dorothy gains possession of the Silver Slippers and their magic becomes accessible for good. Although Dorothy thought she had done something bad by killing the Wicked Witch, through her innate goodness she actually becomes a vehicle to transform evil.

Oftentimes we are unable to see the value of a particularly uncomfortable feeling or situation until we catch a glimpse of a bigger picture, then the value of our hardships becomes clear. As we settle into recognition of the higher order of things, it is easier to accept our personal struggles, knowing that they contribute in some way to the higher good of everyone.

When catapulted into tumultuous experiences, unexpected support and serendipitous assistance often come our way. It is as though surrendering to life's catastrophes allows the blessings of divine intervention to manifest themselves. These surprising moments inspire and empower us to continue through the hardships of our journey.

Just as Dorothy was protected in Oz, when I began to consciously embrace a spiritual path, I too felt divinely protected and supported. I remember walking alone one afternoon in quiet desperation on a deserted beach. In the depths of my solitude, the surf gently and surprisingly washed up a bright red flower at my feet that broke the spell of my depression. Later when I was driving carefully down a mountain road covered with ice and snow, my car spun out of control as I rounded a treacherous curve. I stopped a few feet from the edge of a steep cliff and watched in horror as cars skidded around me. Somehow there were no accidents that day. I gratefully continued my journey, humbled by the mystery of divine intercession.

The rational mind balks at the thought of divine protection, or the power of a witch's kiss. However, as we explore life experiences and open to the wondrous worlds of invisible phenomena, another order reveals itself that is beyond the confines of logic and reason.

When Dorothy turns to the Good Witch of the North and asks how to begin the journey, she is told to simply "Begin at the beginning." Often in our excitement to embark on a new adventure or direction in life, we reject the ordinariness of simple beginnings and jump enthusiastically into complex and confusing situations. As Dorothy demonstrates, this is not the best way to arrive home. She models for us how an unsophisticated farm girl, without any supernatural powers or extraordinary gifts continues diligently, step by step, until she reaches her destination.

Patience is one of the first and most difficult virtues to cultivate on our journey. We often grow irritated with the rhythm of the universe and push impatiently against it. We can exhaust ourselves with our efforts though, and become frustrated with the ineffectiveness of trying to control our experiences. One of Dorothy's most valuable lessons is to accept the strange ways of life and persistently face its challenges.

When Dorothy arrives in Oz, she acquires the powerful Silver Shoes almost immediately. The Good Witch of the North encourages her to wear them, and it is these Silver Slippers that eventually carry her home. Shoes are seen throughout the world as signs of liberty, freedom, and power. Slaves are forbidden to wear them, perhaps as an indication of their bondage and servitude. In many places, shoes are removed before entering a house as a sign of respect and submissiveness. The soles of our shoes act as intermediaries between our feet and the ground. They provide the platform on which we stand, allow movement in the world without injury to the body, and show us the importance of connecting our souls with Mother Earth. Through our soles we are reminded of our relationship with the earth and the importance of being grounded in the world. Although the shoes are believed to be powerful, neither Dorothy nor the Good Witch knows how to use them. They are essential for Dorothy's journey home, and intuitively she defends her right to them when the Wicked Witch tries to take them away from her.

A journey suggests movement in the world. On a physical level, this means setting one foot in front of the other and staying in motion. As the Good Witch says when Dorothy asks her how to find the Wizard, "You must begin at the beginning." In order to find our way home we must walk the path of awareness carefully, step by step, moment by moment, absorbing the wisdom of the earth and expanding into the spaciousness of the sky. Ironically, when a person stands still there is an opportunity for quiet and relaxation.

This allows outward movement to continue inwards, and creates a shift that exposes interior worlds and reveals unexpected treasures. If our energy is moving outwards constantly, we cannot discover these hidden gems. It is the feet that carry us forward, and the feet that bring us to a stand still. They are the vehicles for our journey and point us in the direction of our search.

Silver is the color of the moon which is associated with the feminine, and more particularly with virgins and purity. It represents fertility, universal becoming, perpetual renewal, and immortality. Silver emerges with the refinement of ore, and alchemists recognize it as a precursor for the appearance of gold. In Christian traditions silver symbolizes the purification of the soul. The fact that the magical Slippers are silver may suggest that Dorothy is emerging from the innocence of childhood and learning to express the golden aspects of her femininity that will lead to her maturity as a woman.

The Silver Slippers represent the internal wisdom of feminine intuition. With their introduction at the beginning of the story, there is an implication that the full manifestation of feminine power has not yet occurred. The potential is hidden, as if a seed awaiting birth. When Dorothy enters the story, she is ignorant of her wisdom as a woman and lacking in self-knowledge and understanding. In protecting the Silver Slippers and confronting the Wicked Witch, she accesses these powers and develops an independent sense of herself. The completion of this process allows her to return home.

CHAPTER FIVE

DOROTHY'S TRAVELING COMPANIONS

So once more the little company set off upon the journey, the Lion walking with stately strides at Dorothy's side.
L. Frank Baum, *The Wonderful Wizard of Oz*, Chapter IV

In her travels through Oz Dorothy befriends many unusual characters. A talking scarecrow, a man made of tin, and a cowardly lion reflect the diversity and uniqueness of this strange land. Just like foreigners who find their refuge in America, Oz is a haven for a plethora of unique individuals. Dorothy's innocent acceptance of these characters creates a bond of friendship that becomes essential for her survival. Her lack of fear and prejudice is a simple expression of the strength and love that develop with the harmonious integration of diversity.

Symbolically this fairy tale describes how a person becomes healed and whole. The Scarecrow, the Tin Woodman, and the Cowardly Lion represent unexplored, wounded, and undeveloped aspects of the psyche. As the travelers evolve together, they create a state of integration and wholeness that leads Dorothy into a more conscious awareness of herself. Through this inner development, she returns home to a place of contentment and self-realization. Traveling in Oz is like journeying into the irrational world of the unconscious. Things are not always as they appear. Although the Scarecrow, the Tin Woodman, and the Cowardly Lion seem to be characters in their own right, they exist only in

Oz. Symbolically they represent the internal aspects of Dorothy's developing psyche.

Psychological growth involves exploring the contents of the unconscious and accepting the often confusing material that resides there. Baum's fairy tale encourages us to do this by focusing our attention on aspects of the personality that usually remain hidden. As we become aware of these hidden characteristics, a realistic and more conscious sense of who we are emerges. Acceptance of these traits creates an internal experience of transformation and awakening. The continuing expansion of this burgeoning awareness allows the intuitive wisdom and understanding of the unconscious to emerge.

When I began to consciously pursue the development of my own psyche, I was a very logical, skeptical, and guarded person. I functioned with a strong ego that maintained a rigid and defensive posture in the world. Although I was quite competent and creative in my accomplishments, internally I felt confused, constricted, and filled with self-doubt. Like Dorothy, I yearned to be relaxed and at home within myself, and thought that rigorously improving internal attitudes and modifying personality characteristics would create inner peace. With an outward show of self-confidence and competence, I often jumped into new situations without hesitation, and then later had to learn the necessary skills to function successfully. Although I usually rose to the occasion, I lived with a constant fear that I would be unable to fulfill the expectations I had placed on myself.

When I first began working as a psychotherapist, I had a supervisor who insisted I give public presentations. I was quite terrified of speaking to large gatherings, and worried that the incompetence I felt internally would become obvious to everyone, shattering my credibility as a professional. Although I received outstanding feedback as a teacher and presenter, I was unable to free myself from the chains of my own anxiety. I worked meticulously to improve my self-confidence, but it was not until I relaxed into a deeper state of self-acceptance and dropped the need to prove myself, that things began to shift.

While traveling the Yellow Brick Road of life, I have been forced to examine many painful areas like this, that I had repressed behind an attitude of self-righteous confidence. Just like the inadequacies of the Scarecrow, the Tin Woodman, and the Cowardly Lion, blind spots limited my understanding, fears constricted my heart, and insecurities motivated my self-righteous attitudes. As I began to accept these dysfunctional attitudes within myself, I experienced the healing that comes with lovingly exposing and embracing all aspects of myself. When I reflect on *The Wonderful Wizard of Oz*, I appreciate more fully the depth and importance of Dorothy's relationship with the Scarecrow, the Tin Woodman, and the Cowardly Lion.

THE SCARECROW WITHIN

The first character Dorothy meets as she travels the Yellow Brick Road is a talking scarecrow stranded in a cornfield. He is distraught because he cannot scare away crows successfully. He blames his incompetence on the inability to think and bemoans the fact that he has no brains. He is caught literally at a crossroads until Dorothy arrives to give him direction and mobility.

Scarecrows are placed in fields to protect growing seedlings and ensure fruitful harvests. They are stretched between the horizontal plane of Mother Earth and the vertical plane of Father Sky, dangling precariously on a cross that intersects these two domains. Although crosses show the descent of spirit into matter, they also demonstrate the polarity of two intersecting directions. The Scarecrow is stuck on a pole and unable to move forward in his life. In the MGM movie, he points one way and then the other before folding his arms across his chest in utter bewilderment. He is delighted and relieved when Dorothy pulls him off his uncomfortable perch and indicates a viable direction for him to travel.

People often project onto others what they are unable to acknowledge in themselves. For example, a person who feels insecure about their intelligence is quick to notice faults in another person's thinking. Dorothy hears the Scarecrow's cries for help shortly after she arrives in Oz. She is a victim of circumstances beyond her control and feels powerless to effect any change in her life. She quickly sees the helplessness of the Scarecrow's situation and empathizes with his inability to function successfully. Perhaps like the Scarecrow, Dorothy is also feeling stuck and in need of brains. If she knew the way back to Kansas she would be able to return home.

The presence of a brain suggests the ability to assimilate information correctly, reason accurately, follow intuitive inclinations creatively, and communicate clearly. It is a complex organ composed of different regions that regulate various bodily functions. Much research has focused on the diverse activity of the brain's right and left hemispheres. The left side controls language, logic, and reasoning. It organizes and categorizes information. The right hemisphere regulates and records emotions, intuitive ideas, and creative correlations. Both hemispheres of the brain must be engaged to eliminate confusion and activate creative potential.

Dorothy travels in Oz as our personal representative. Her encounter with the Scarecrow suggests that there is an aspect of our own psyche in need of attention. In the area of the intellect, our culture has become unbalanced. Although all functions of the brain are essential for our survival, we glorify the attributes of the left hemisphere and discount the significance of the right. The traditionally feminine traits of intuition, sensitivity, and receptivity are judged inferior and undesirable, while the masculine ones of rational thought and analytical reasoning are considered stronger and more valuable. The separation and judgment of these traits fuels the anxiety and inner chaos experienced by many individuals today.

The Scarecrow's healing comes with the recognition of his own intelligence, just as a spilt psyche mends when the neglected aspects of the intellect are acknowledged and valued. The Scarecrow's inability to function successfully emphasizes the importance of reclaiming the right-brain functions. It is not until all aspects of the intellect have been activated that awareness, understanding, and wisdom are free to develop. It is crucial for the whole brain to be functioning harmoniously for a person to move in the world effectively.

When the Wizard bestows new brains on the Scarecrow after the death of the Wicked Witch of the West, his comments remind us that "Experience is the only thing that brings knowledge, and the longer you are on the earth the more experience you are sure to get." Wisdom does not come directly from knowledge or information stored in the mind. It is not acquired from another person or learned in a textbook. We must engage with life wholeheartedly to reap the benefits of our experiences. Cultivating awareness of actions, thoughts, and feelings allows expansion beyond the confines of the rational mind. This awareness activates the intuitive capabilities of the brain, and develops a matrix of understanding and wisdom that underlies all experience.

A number of years ago, a friend helped bring the Scarecrow aspects of myself into consciousness. He was an artist and musician, and lived his life spontaneously and exuberantly. I had repressed the playful functioning of my right brain and lived in a very controlled and serious manner. By eliminating my appointment book and following the flow of my own creative energy, my attitude relaxed and the restrictive conditioning that had dominated my life diminished. His presence gave me permission to lighten my burden of self-assumed responsibilities and respect the voice of my intuitive inclinations. As a result, feelings of indecision and confusion vanished, and I found myself living with increased self-confidence, clarity, and understanding.

Years ago a young woman came into my office confused and angry with herself for repeating a pattern of choosing married men as romantic partners. She shared several stories of painfully breaking up with a married partner, promising herself never to repeat this pattern, and then "falling in love" with another unavailable man. She immediately told me that she was not interested in looking at her past, and wanted to find a way to stop this self-destructive behavior. She reminded me of the Scarecrow, stuck on a pole, and unable to function successfully. Although she knew what to do, she could not mobilize herself to act accordingly. She came from a family of substance abusers, and her parents bounced her back and forth through their stormy divorce with accompanying emotional abuse. It was many months before she could trust me and open to her inner experience, and many more months before she was willing to explore the confusion of her early childhood experiences. As we patiently examined the sources of her conditioning, she was able to appreciate the depth and pain of her inner struggles. With self-acceptance and insight, her understanding and compassion grew, and she began to make healthier choices in her relationships.

THE TIN WOODMAN WITHIN

As Dorothy continues her journey, she discovers a man made of tin immobilized in a forest. He is caught in a rainstorm and rusts before he reaches his oilcan. As L. Frank Baum explains, the Tin Woodman was originally a man of flesh and bold. He was in love with a young woman who lived in a forest with an old witch. When the witch discovered the romance, she enchanted the woodchopper's axe. As he worked the axe attacked him, striking first at his arms and legs. He found a tinsmith to replace his cut-off limbs, but the axe continued to strike at him and eventually his whole body was made of metal. Tragically, the tinsmith forgot to give the woodchopper a heart, and the Tin Woodman no longer felt love for his sweetheart. He longs for a new heart so he can know the delights of love once again.

Just as the Scarecrow represents one aspect of the wounded male to be rescued by the feminine, the Tin Woodman represents another. Here we have a man put under a spell by a possessive and powerful witch. He is blinded by love and unaware of the destructive powers of a vengeful woman. The witch's sorcery forces him to become a victim of his own weapon of aggression.

The Tin Woodman represents the disconnection that occurs within the psyche when emotions are denied and suppressed. People who experience blocked feelings for many years, often suffer with stiff and tense bodies. Their physical musculature becomes an armor of protection from the emotional undulations of life. They live in a cold, calculating, and painfully isolated world, untouched by the warmth of a loving heart.

The Tin Woodman is a man of action, an aggressor who must learn to feel again. Wounded by the violent nature of his occupation, he is frozen with the belief that he can no longer experience love. When aggression gets out of control, it threatens all involved. We become hard and tough in order to shelter our softer vulnerabilities. Only when the environment appears safe and respectful, do we emerge from our protected space and open our hearts to others.

I am reminded of a man who came to me for therapy because his marriage had failed. He was a successful attorney, devoted to his work and zealous in his dedication to physical fitness. Although he was in excellent shape, he would not allow his hardened body to be touched, and lived in an isolated shell that prevented intimacy. He had been single for many years, and was frustrated because he could not sustain a long-term relationship. His current girlfriend was complaining about his lack of emotional availability, and he was eager to move beyond his fears into a fulfilling romance.

This situation is similar to many men who are functioning successfully in the business world, and unable to participate in intimate love relationships. It was many months before he was able to open up and recognize the basis of his fears, and many more months before he could trust enough to share openly his pain and vulnerability. He had to give up his rigid ideas of success and control, and surrender to the emotional inconsistencies and irrational reactivity of his own heart. With time, and cradled in an environment of loving acceptance, he was able to open the tender places within himself and deepen into a loving and committed relationship.

The Tin Woodman is a startling reminder of the value of love. It is ironical that this fictional character made of metal harbors such a burning desire for a heart. Although he appears stiff and rigid, in the nurturing presence of a loving woman, he is free to express the compassion and tenderness that reside within his armor of metal. The Tin Woodman encourages us to respect our feelings of love and tenderness, and honor the importance of heartfelt connections.

The Wizard doubts the value of a heart because, "It makes most people unhappy." Opening to love means accepting all our emotions, the painful as well as the blissful ones. As the Tin Woodman reminds us, it is important to keep ourselves well oiled and to let feelings flow freely so our hearts can continue to experience the joys of love.

In a strange twist of roles, it was a loving man who opened my heart after it had broken and closed after the ending of a particularly difficult relationship. Although I was distrustful at first, Peter's unconditional and pervasive love slowly melted my fears and loosened my joints so that I could move freely in the world and like the Tin Woodman, feel love once again.

THE COWARDLY LION WITHIN

The next creature Dorothy meets as she travels along the Yellow Brick Road is a lion who is afraid to take his rightful place as king of the jungle. Other animals intimidate him, and his fears prevent him from facing any confrontation. When he attacks Toto, an animal much smaller than himself, Dorothy is horrified. She admonishes him strongly, and his threatening attitude dissolves into a tearful admission of his feelings of inadequacy. Once again Dorothy initiates healing for a wounded male character who is unable to function successfully.

Although it is natural to be afraid when there is danger, the Cowardly Lion lives in a constant state of agitation that resembles a neurotic mind. He distorts reality by creating imaginary fears that perpetuate self-doubt and insecurity. In an effort to compensate for his lack of confidence, he adopts an inflated and pretentious attitude that Dorothy shatters quite easily with a simple slap on the nose. He becomes naked and vulnerable in the presence of the feminine, dropping his defenses and exposing his soul's torment.

Lions are traditionally associated with royalty. In their natural state they are considered brave, bold, strong, and at the top of the food chain. They live comfortably in the wild and function with alertness, confidence, and ease. The lion's graceful embodiment of power, physical strength, and attentiveness is an inspiration for the balance of mind, body, and spirit that comes with inner freedom and unencumbered living.

The zodiac sign of Leo the Lion represents creativity, leadership, and the sun. Lions stand proudly on the British coat of arms, and crowned with a pharaoh's head, they form majestic sphinxes in Egypt. Lions are credited with healing properties and goddess worship. Their long flowing manes bring to mind the strength and power contained in the hair of the biblical hero Samson.

Although lions suggest bravery, generosity, and courage, they also represent the less desirable qualities of pomposity, overindulgence, and egotism. They are a gentle reminder that people in leadership positions must be vigilant in their use of power. Without awareness, it is easy to become domineering, greedy, and insensitive to the needs of others. When a lion enters the symbolic life of a person, issues relating to power, instincts, and passion often arise.

Courage is an essential attitude that enables the development of love, trust, and truthfulness. It allows us to bypass our defensive reactions, so that we can inquire into the nature of reality and fearlessly venture into the unknown. Without courage, the heart is unable to open and the mind cannot recognize the truth. Cowards rarely explore beyond the world they already know. I am reminded of a time I was preparing for a particularly challenging presentation, when a friend embraced me with well wishes and lovingly placed a Cowardly Lion figure in my hand. This simple gift brought a smile to my lips and dissolved the clutches of fear that were paralyzing me.

It is easy to recognize our neurotic fears through the Cowardly Lion's pretentious displays of bravado. Only in the presence of unconditional love can we relax and dissolve these protective façades. Then the self-doubts and insecurities buried within the psyche can come into the light and be healed. Although it is normal to fear danger, the intense anxiety of the Cowardly Lion prevents him from relating to others normally. As the Wizard reminds him, "All you need is confidence in yourself. There is no living thing that is not afraid when it faces danger. True courage is in facing danger when you are afraid and that kind of courage you have in plenty."

As a small child, I was particularly fascinated with the Cowardly Lion. Hours disappeared as I studied his image and contemplated his existence. He reminded me of myself – bold and ferocious on the outside, timid and scared on the inside. I began to realize that everyone has a hidden inner self and an outer personality. I could see it in others just as I could in myself. Many times in my past this ability to see beyond the personality into a person's inner world created confusion and disturbance. I was mystified by the games people played and the façades they hid behind. I would see the beauty and good intentions of a person's heart, and be unable to recognize the inflated or self-defeating attitudes they had adopted. I took what they said at face value, and was mystified when their promises dissolved like the Wizard's hot air balloon. In my young adult years, I found myself on the edge of social gatherings waiting for opportunities to connect with someone beneath the plethora of masks I saw.

It is only in the presence of Dorothy that the Scarecrow, the Tin Woodman, and the Cowardly Lion are able to address their inadequacies. She creates a climate of unconditional love and acceptance that stimulates healing and growth. When we are surrounded with a loving environment, our spirit naturally reveals and heals its psychic wounds. No other self-improvement regimes are necessary.

Dorothy's gentle manner, heartfelt responsiveness, and persistent focus demonstrate the power and importance of the feminine as a healing agent. In the Last Generation Star Trek series, Counselor Troy extols the value of healing in the presence of the feminine. By listening patiently when the Captain expresses confusion, the counselor's accepting and attentive attitude allows the identification of disturbing issues and the clarification of conflicting feelings. Just like Dorothy, the Counselor creates an atmosphere where a person's inadequacies are exposed and healed, so that they can resume functioning successfully. It is reassuring to see the power of feminine intuition and sensitivity being honored so overtly in our culture now, particularly after they have been so denigrated in times past.

CHAPTER SIX
OZ THEMES IN SANDPLAY

I believe that dreams—day dreams you know—with your eyes wide open and your brain machinery whizzing—are likely to lead to the betterment of the world.
    L. Frank Baum, *The Lost Princess of Oz*, To My Readers

Before the days of printing presses and move houses, storytelling was a basic form of entertainment. Folk tales, legends, myths, and fairy tales were shared eagerly among adults and children. Repeated recitation helped preserve the values, ideals, and beliefs of the culture from which they originated. *The Wonderful Wizard of Oz* is one of these lovable stories that have become an integral part of American society. Many now consider it the quintessential American fairy tale, and it exemplifies the values and ideals of our culture.

Fairy tales are treasured for their ability to spark new ideas, inspire creative solutions, and magically transform the quality of life. Through awakening the imagination, they act as doorways into the realm of the unconscious. The actions of their heroes demonstrate inner states of mind that instill hope, reassurance, and the possibility of happy endings. Fairy tales allow us to dance in a world of make-believe and fantasy with the wide-eyed innocence of children. L. Frank Baum speaks eloquently about this in *The Lost Princess of Oz.*

Imagination has brought mankind through the Dark Ages to its present state of civilization. Imagination led

Columbus to discover America. Imagination led Franklin to discover electricity. Imagination has given us the steam engine, the telephone, the talking machine and the automobile, for these things had to be dreamed of before they became realities. The imaginative child will become the imaginative man or woman most apt to create, to invent, and therefore to foster civilization. A prominent educator tells me that fairy tales are of untold value in developing imagination in the young. I believe, it. (Baum, *The Lost Princess of Oz*, 1917)

USE OF SYMBOLIC IMAGERY

Images from the Oz story are often used as metaphors to describe particular aspects of an individual's inner growth. When the rational mind is unable to resolve internal distress, fantasy stories and visual imagery can depict confused feelings and attitudes much more effectively than verbal descriptions. Words such as happy, sad, or brave pale in comparison to images created with metaphor and story. Shimmering fairies dancing on rainbows of delight, rivers of sadness washing away pain, lions courageously leaping over bottomless ravines, or lines drawn in sand stimulate us to experience emotions directly. Although inner sensations cannot be verbalized easily, symbolic language allows their expression by conjuring images that can be shared. Communicating in this way creates an atmosphere that fosters deep communion and profound understanding among people.

As with any significant myth or fairy tale, the Oz story has been used over and over in a myriad of ways. This is how archetypal energies become integrated into the lives and psyches of individuals. When mythical stories first appear in a culture, their meaning and significance is often overlooked. People respond to them strongly, but usually do to understand the power of their attraction. They are experienced as entertaining and appealing, but their deeper meaning is not consciously recognized. As the

universal thoughts contained within these tales come into awareness, their hidden messages can be digested and absorbed into an
individual's life.

SANDPLAY THERAPY

When I first began to work as a psychotherapist, I was quite skeptical
of the theories I had been taught about the inner world. I adopted
a pragmatic and practical approach to therapy, and only believed
what I could experience or observe directly. In the process of my
training I had learned to conduct psychological evaluations, and
became competent in the assessment of a person's emotional, intel-
lectual, and personality functioning. Although many of the proce-
dures I used were standardized and objective, the process included
what are called projective techniques. These are composed of various kinds of creative drawings and stories that provide a way for a
person to describe what they are experiencing internally without
using the traditional approach of verbal words. I became intrigued
with the use of symbolic language, and the wealth of information
that could be shared in this way. Drawing, collage, clay, story telling,
puppetry, and therapeutic play became an intricate part of my work
with both children and adults, as I moved away from traditional
models for psychotherapy.

Coupled with an interest in the expressive arts was my growing exploration of meditation and spirituality. As I deepened in my
work as a psychotherapist, I began to see that although psychological growth is important it cannot carry a person all the way home
to a place of inner peace and harmony. It had been my burning
desire to find the key to peace and happiness, so as I began to recognize the limitations of my profession, I dedicated myself with
renewed vigor to my spiritual quest. I spent months in silent retreats
with active and silent meditations, embraced the teachings of the
Buddha and incorporated them into my life, pursued my interest
in yoga with enthusiasm, and delighted in the wisdom of awakened
teachers from around the world.

It was my mother who suggested I look into Sandplay as a therapeutic model that would resonate with my spiritual and psychological interests. I attended a conference with her, and then began my own process to see what this technique could offer. I had made a promise to myself at the beginning of my training that I would never ask anyone to do anything I had not done myself. You can imagine the plethora of personal growth experiences I have undertaken as a result of this commitment. I am convinced that healers must discover what is valuable through their own personal experience, especially in the area of psycho-spiritual functioning.

I entered Sandplay therapy with enthusiasm, eager to see what it could offer, and was astounded at the depth to which this process could identify and heal internal pain and confusion. As I addressed problematic areas within myself through Sandplay, things in my life began to change. I was seen and acknowledged in a way that freed me to pursue my destiny without encumbrance.

Sandplay is a therapeutic approach that was developed by Dora Kalff almost 50 years ago under the guidance of Dr. Carl Jung. It is a direct method to experience the self, which Jung encouraged as an essential step for healthy development. Through this sacred process, the unconscious emerges spontaneously and inner wisdom becomes accessible.

In my office, two walls of shelves are covered with miniature figures and forms of every type imaginable. People, animals, birds, reptiles, houses, boats, trains, cars, trees flowers, rocks, fairies, angels, gods, goddesses, fairy tale characters, and more, crowd onto these shelves and seduce observers into the world of symbolic play. I also provide two small sand boxes in which figures can be placed to create scenes and tell stories about the inner world.

Often times it is easier to communicate through symbols in a sand tray than to communicate verbally. Feelings do not translate directly into words, but an arrangement of different images can easily convey the complexities of the inner world. Just expressing and sharing

Sandplay Shelves

emotional pain and confusion can be healing for the soul. When a person sees their own creation in the sand it deepens this healing, and helps to clarify their problem and identify what to do. Working in the sand allows a person to view with conscious awareness, aspects of themselves that have been buried in the unconscious. As this material rises to consciousness, repressed blocks are released, and choices made with expanded consciousness are possible.

SOMEWHERE OVER THE RAINBOW

One of the best-known references to the rainbow in our times occurs in *The Wizard of Oz*. Although not part of Baum's original story, Judy Garland's singing of "Somewhere Over the Rainbow" suggests that dreams may come true in a land beyond the rainbow, where birds fly freely and "clouds are far behind me." Although the Land of Oz is not problem free, Dorothy's ability to overcome challenges and obtain her heart's desire reinforces the hope that rewards will come with persistent effort and determination. Rainbows are one of the most beautiful and majestic manifestations of pure light that can be perceived on the physical plane. When a rainbow's pathway of color crosses the sky, it creates a breathtaking spectacle and inspires a sense of wonder and awe. After a rainstorm, the rainbow's presence seems to emanate an uplifting reminder of hope and the renewal of life. It stimulates the imagination and suggests that the clear luminescence of the sun is not far behind the storm clouds of doubt and confusion.

Mary is a 41-year old woman who was physically abused by her mother as a child and sexually molested throughout her teen-age years by her brother and his friends. Her father, to whom she felt emotionally close, died when she was 12 years old. As a young adult, she became very involved with a fundamentalist Christian religion and married a man with similar beliefs. She has been emotionally abused and unhappy in her marriage, but has had difficulty taking action because of her religious conviction. Through years of therapy, Mary has healed her childhood wounds and developed a successful career. Currently she is struggling with a desire to leave her marriage and the conflicts that arise because her commitment to the church.

Sand Scene 6-1

In this Sandplay (Sand Scene 6-1), done after many months of therapy, Mary depicts the strengths that have developed in her life, as well as the areas that remain to be explored. This dual focus is demonstrated graphically with her use of the rainbow, which shows what is coming into consciousness for her. At one end of the bow she placed a heart, a symbol of her desire to manifest love in her life. At the other end is a key that points to what she describes as the "dark side of the tray." In this area there are two men: one who "looks like he's on a journey" and the other who "appears very serene and peaceful." Although she does not mention the rainbow directly, it seems that the key to her desire to love openly lies in the exploration of her more primitive and instinctual impulses, as represented by the African man. In this tray, the colors of the rainbow may indicate the journey which Mary must undertake to achieve a sense of wholeness. Perhaps the presence of the rainbow also promises a harmonious resolution for her spiritual conflict and portends a successful integration of these aspects of her personality.

Sand Scene 6-2

In her next Sandplay (Fig 6-2), completed about six weeks later, Mary again used the symbol of the rainbow, describing it as a "promise." This tray she said, represents her desire for "unity with others" and the "birth of something new in my life." She felt very hopeful and positive about resolving her conflicts and moving through this difficult period of internal distress. Although the scene appears peaceful and uplifting, she carefully roughed up the sand, stating that "everything's not smooth and easy. The waters are still stormy and difficult." It seems that the journey of integration suggested by the direction of the key in the previous tray is just beginning. Mary is more conscious and accepting of the struggle facing her, and shows her anticipation of a successful outcome by placing the rainbow in this tray.

Laura is a 44-year-old woman who sought therapy to resolve the self-destructive patterns she has been repeating in intimate relationships. Raised primarily by her mother, her father died before she was born and her mother did not remarry until she was 9 years old. Laura has been divorced for 14 years, and has had numerous relationships with men since that time. She lives alone and recently returned to school to obtain a master's degree.

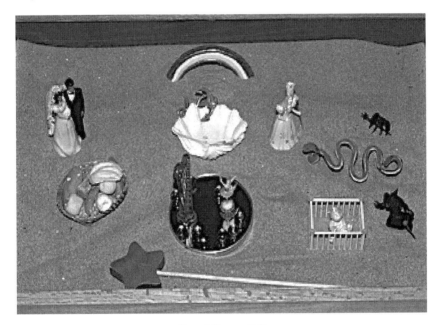

Sand Scene 6-3

In therapy, Laura has been exploring her feelings towards her mother, whom she perceives as a very critical and negative woman. In her fifth Sandplay (Sand Scene 6-3), she represents this negative mother graphically by depicting a witch threatening a baby in a crib. She placed what she considers to be negative symbols on one side of the tray and positive symbols on the other, bridging them with a rainbow. In the center of the tray, in front of the rainbow, she put a mirror, a wand, and a shell with water. Apparently these are the elements she needs to achieve self-awareness and unification of her light and dark sides. The rainbow is the bridge that unites these two polarities and suggests the areas that need to be developed in order for integration to occur.

Sand Scene 6-4

In her next session (Sand Scene 6-4), Laura describes the rainbow as being "above it all" and "in the heavens, covering everything." In the rest of the tray she depicts the chaos of her life, with all the elements intermixed. It seems the Aborigine's rainbow serpent has swallowed the chaos of Laura's life and spewed it out again. Perhaps through this process the elements of her life can be reordered and a transformation can occur.

Sand Scene 6-5

In the next tray (Sand Scene 6-5), which was done one week later, the rainbow has risen higher in the tray, and order has been established. Laura has confined the "messy part of my life" to the lower front of the tray, and a number of gods and goddesses are placed in the chaos to assist her with "cleaning things up." The rainbow acts as an umbrella for this activity, promising the reward of a successful relationship as seen with the bride and groom. When she completes her cleaning, self-manifestation is also possible as seen with the mirror.

Sand Scene 6-6

This next sand scene (Sand Scene 6-6) most closely resembles the rainbow Judy Garland sang about at the beginning of *The Wizard of Oz*. Here a 35-year-old woman creates a picture of she and her husband crossing a bridge together into a new stage in their relationship. They had both been through a period of intense personal growth and career changes, and were exploring how to integrate these changes into their relationship. When Catherine observed this scene, she felt hopeful that they would be able to reconcile their differences and find a way to enter into this new territory together. Although snow-covered trees surround them, they are leaving the forest behind and approaching new territory that is well lit with a candle. Success seems quite hopeful with the presence of the rainbow.

Like all symbols, the presence of a rainbow in a particular sand tray can carry many different meanings. It may be used as a bridge connecting the two divergent areas within a person's psyche, or it may indicate an area of the psyche that needs to be developed so that integration can occur. Australian Aborigine myths describe the rainbow as a serpent that has the power to create and destroy by swallowing people and earth forms into its great womb and then regurgitating them to give birth to new creations. A rainbow in a person's tray may be representing this transformative force that rearranges all the elements of a person's life and stimulates the creation of a stable foundation within the psyche. Finally, a rainbow is often selected for the tray to signify the hope or promise that when the hard work is complete, a sense of personal contentment and happiness will emerge. In alignment with the Oz story, the rainbow holds a promise of success for Dorothy, suggesting a place where happiness and contentment do exist. In retrospect, it foretells the transformation that will occur with her journey through Oz.

FOLLOW THE YELLOW BRICK ROAD

A 22-year-old woman created figure 6-7 with two small children who was dissatisfied with her marriage and questioning the direction of her life. In one of her first sandplays, she placed a Yellow Brick Road in the center of the tray, with a ballerina at one end and naked women covering her eyes at the other. Along the road are a little girl and a scary monster-like man, and in the background are a snake, a house, blue horses, blue stones, trees and shells. Sophia worked with determination in her therapy, obtained a job that would support her children, divorced her husband, and returned to school to pursue a career direction. Two years later she created Sand Scene 6-8. Often the psyche will recreate a powerful image and with a few changes reveal the transformation that has occurred internally. Here the Yellow Brick Road is placed in the same position in the tray, and the naked woman is replaced with a golden tree. There is a sense of abundance and fulfillment, and although there are still issues to resolve, this scene indicates there has been a tremendous shift in her inner world.

Sand Scene 6-7

Sand Scene 6-8

These scenes (Sand Scene 6-9 & 6-10) were done by a 28-year-old recovering alcoholic who was active in AA and committed to working a twelve-step program. He had been raised by an abusive alcoholic father, and although he was angry and hurt in this relationship, he was eager to obtain his father's approval and acceptance. In the sand he created a Yellow Brick Road that ran through two trays placed end to end. He represents hardships along the way in the first tray, and then connects the two trays with a bridge. In the second tray (Sand Scene 6-10), the bridge leads to two men lying in the sand side by side. He describes these figures as he and his father, and is excited to realize that there is a reconciliation emerging. As he deepened with his therapy, layers of discontent and self-destructive attitudes and behaviors dropped away. About 8 months after the first tray, he created the scene in Sand Scene 6-11. Here the Yellow Brick Road expands to surround four pairs of men relating in different ways. Although he had been in relationships with women most of his life, recently this man had realized that he was primarily attracted to men. This recognition flooded him with relief, and he entered a gay relationship soon after this. Although he was not able to admit his sexual preference earlier, perhaps his unconscious was attempting to communicate with him through the sand. He had interpreted that tray as being about his father; in retrospect it seemed to be about his own sexual identity.

Sand Scene 6-9

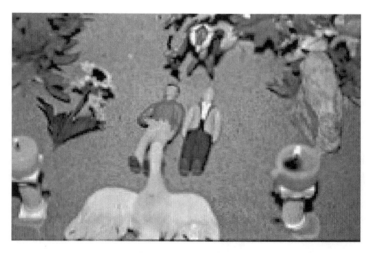

Sand Scene 6-10

Sand Scene 6-11

"I'LL GET YOU MY PRETTY"

Many people use the Wicked Witch to represent negative or threatening feelings about women general or mother's in particular. In the midst of a long series of trays, for a few months this 43-year-old woman entered a dark place in her psyche where she confronted her deepest fears about the witchy women who had tormented her when she was alive. She had just come into a place of realizing her inner beauty, and this seemed to give her the strength she needed to delve deeper into the dark and frightening areas of her inner world. She began to bring witches into her trays, and in Sand Scene 6-12 she raised three of them onto pedestals and placed herself kneeling before them as a naked and venerable woman. A month later, in Sand Scene 6-13, the witches have returned to normal size, and are confronted by a buffalo. No longer is she a victim of these threatening women. She has absorbed the energy of the buffalo and is able to stand strong in the presence of her deepest fears without being overshadowed or destroyed.

Sand Scene 6-12

Sand Scene 6-13

In Sand Scene 6-14, the Wicked Witch is just one of many images of darkness in a tray filled with black objects. In previous trays, this 38-year woman had placed images of light and joy. Now she was sinking into an exploration of her fears and anxieties, and giving an overview of what that felt like to her. As her therapy continued, she worked with the negative feelings around particular issues until she was able to free herself of their hold on her.

Sand Scene 6-14

Sand Scene 6-15 was done by an eleven-year-old girl who was suffering with low self-esteem, compulsive eating; unwillingness to participate in school activates, and fear of sleeping alone in her room. Maggie's parents had divorced a few years earlier, three of her grandparents had died, and her best friend had moved away. We worked together for a year, discussing various situations at work and at home that were troubling her, and exploring different expressive art processes. At one point towards the end of therapy, she entered my office and immediately began to work in the sand. As the scene of Dorothy and her companions emerged, she took great care to lay the objects of their desire near each of them; a barrel for the Scarecrow's brains, a heart for the Tin Woodman, blue beads for the Cowardly Lion's courage, and a silver moon for Dorothy to find her way home. The Wicked Witch is melting in the background, and the Wizard is flying away in his hot air balloon. She placed the tornado near a house with a yellow ball inside, and then carefully drew a line in the sand from corner to corner. It seems that Dorothy and her friends, just like Maggie, have realized their inner resources and confronted their deepest fears, but that the journey home has not yet been completed. Maggie has healed her psychological wounds and recovered from her grief, but still has to make the journey south to Glinda in order to find her way home. The completion of this tray was a milestone for Maggie, and we celebrated the death of the Wicked Witch singing and dancing to the well-known song "Ding dong the Witch is dead."

Sand Scene 6-15

FINDING THE WAY HOME

Finding the way home to an internal state of peace and happiness is a common theme throughout therapy. People arrive at my office in varying states of emotional distress, and are eager to find relief and resolution for their turmoil.

In Sand Scene 6-16 a 35-year-old woman could only share the traumas of an abusive childhood through Sandplay. Her first sand scene showed Dorothy, the Scarecrow, the Tin Woodman, and the Cowardly Lion moving together towards the Wicked Witch, who was lying face down in the front of the tray. My client seemed to be mobilizing her resources to confront and then melt the Wicked Witch. There was also a vulnerable rabbit standing face to face with a terrifying dragon. I imagined this scene as representing the great fear and anxiety my client must have been feeling as she reexamined her painful past. There was a castle in the upper right corner of the tray, and she carefully drew a line in the sand from Dorothy to the doorway, stating that she needed to find her way home. She identified strongly with Dorothy, acknowledging her confrontation with the Wicked Witch and expressing the difficulties that needed to be overcome in her search for home. Later she brought her symbolic communication into real life by resolving disagreements with her mother, confronting an abusive male co-worker, and settling into a new home. Although initially symbolic language can appear mysterious and confusing, when its message is understood awareness and insight increase.

Sand Scene 6-16

Jim is a 55-year-old artist who came to me intrigued with learning more about himself through Sandplay. He was in a committed relationship, and had recently started a business for himself that was flourishing. He was fascinated with *The Wizard of Oz* story, and often spoke of his extensive Oz collection and experiences with other oz-lovers. Although he was not distressed with any particular situation, he did become involved in a confusing legal situation after he began therapy. He was able to express and work through his feelings of anger and frustration about this conflict in the sand, and consequently responded to the accusations that were made with equanimity and wisdom.

Jim decided to meet with me monthly, and created six sand scenes during our time together. His first sandtray, Sand Scene 6-17, was called "My Life in Process." Although there are many things going on throughout the Sandplay series, for simplicity's sake I will only comment on images found in the Oz story.

Sand Scene 6-17

In this scene (Sand Scene 6-17) Jim has laid out the direction of his life. He identified with the wise man on the left, and feeling like the mermaid, he is jumping into the unknown and moving forward through many adventures. Eventually he hopes to find his way home (house) where there is love (heart and loving relationship of Flamingos), wisdom (Yoda), and eternal life (aank). The elevated rainbow is visible from all directions and is creating a climate of hopefulness for the success of his journey. The rainbow at the end of the tray marks the area where he attains his goal of inner harmony.

Sand Scene6-18

The next scene (Sand Scene 6-18) Jim calls "Honoring and Protecting What I Cherish." A legal conflict has erupted unexpectedly in his life and he is angry and concerned about protecting himself. In this scene there are four Wicked Witches; three are flanked with a Flying Monkey and the other has a multi-headed dragon at her side. Dorothy and two Glindas and are part of a protective circle that surrounds a naked infant. The light of consciousness represented by the sun, shines strongly into the center of the circle. Jim was quite relieved to see the strength of his resources as they manifested in the tray. In spite of the threatening Witches, at this point he appears to be feeling safe and unharmed. After this tray

Jim was able to relax, concentrate on an appropriate response to the situation, and examine the lessons he was being offered with this struggle.

Sand Scene 6-19

One month later Jim created Sand Scene 6-19. In this scene the Scarecrow, the Tin Woodman, and the Cowardly Lion are emerging from an opened tool chest filled with blue stones. Dorothy's red shoes are nearby, a rainbow in the center of the tray spans a golden bridge, and at the end of the tray two houses are cradled between two meditating women and other nurturing images. The Wicked Witches and flying Monkey stand before a fire and the powerful Minoan Snake Goddess stands behind them as she did in the previous tray. Jim is feeling good with how he is handling his legal affairs, and describes his toolbox as filled with courage, compassion, and wisdom. He had explicitly asked for spiritual assistance, and now sees himself surrounded with the support needed to lead him home.

In his next scene (Sand Scene 6-20) two Wicked Witches are held off by fighting lions. Dorothy stands on top of a rainbow, and has traveled through another one at her back to emerge from past conflicts safely. The red slippers are at her feet, and her protectors line up behind her. Yoda, a symbol for the inner wisdom that Jim is developing, is in the very center of the tray surrounded with benevolent goddesses. Jim described this tray as a victorious parade with Dorothy in the lead.

Sand Scene 6-20

The next time I saw Jim his legal affairs had been resolved and he was excited about expanding his business. He called Sand Scene

6-21 the "Celebration of a Journey." The Wicked Witch is at the front of the scene, hidden in the trees. Dorothy is in possession of the Witch's broomstick though, and the evil woman is no longer a menacing threat. Through an archway is a road of blue stones, lined with images of Dorothy, Glinda, Yoda, and Aladdin's genie. It leads into an area where gods and goddesses dance beneath the sun and stars, and a rainbow.

Sand Scene 6-21

In his last sand scene (Sand Scene 6-22), titled "New Adventure," Jim has buried the heads of the three Wicked Witches behind a screen. A labyrinth is in the center of the tray, with Dorothy's red shoes in the middle and a rainbow nearby. Dorothy, Glinda and Yoda stand together and all is bathed in the sunlight of consciousness. Although Jim's journey into consciousness continues, he has passed through a particularly challenging time and opened a doorway into new territory within himself. The Oz figures and all that they represent for him have been helpful guides throughout this phase of the journey.

Sand Scene 6-22

CHAPTER SEVEN

DOROTHY AND HER FRIENDS FIND THE SAND

My greatest wish now is to get back to Kansas, for Aunt Em will surely think something dreadful has happened to me, and that will make her put on mourning; and unless the crops are better this year than they were last I am sure Uncle Henry cannot afford it.
L. Frank Baum, *The Wonderful Wizard of Oz*, Chapter XXIII

The characters from Oz are powerful representations of a person's internal concerns. Dorothy, the Scarecrow, the Tin Woodman, the Cowardly Lion, witches and wizards, Yellow Brick Roads, and Ruby Red or Silver Sippers are beautiful ways to express common issues within everyone's psyche. Sandplay gives us a clear idea of what particular images mean. It is easy to understand form the following examples how and why the Oz story has touched so many people over the last hundred years. The tremendous contribution of Sandplay is that we can see how images are used, without any preconceptions about their meaning. As we correlate the scenes that are created with the events of a person's life, the richness of this tool as a communication device becomes obvious, and the personal and collective power of the Oz metaphor becomes undeniable.

The issues that come up for an individual during a Sandplay process are complex and varied. They emerge over many months and are resolved as the psyche incorporates the new information that emerges. Although each sand scene carries a particular message, its full impact is reduced when it is taken out of context. Please remember this as you examine the following scenes.

DOROTHY

The image of Dorothy often appears in a Sandplay when a person is beginning a journey. As a simple Kansas farm girl entering new territory, she embodies the feelings of many people at the beginning of a therapy process. Her presence carries the implication that the process will be successful, even though there may be difficulties along the way.

Sand Scene 7-1

This tray (Sand Scene 7-1) was created by a man in his mid-forties, who described his picture as "the anxieties I'm feeling overall." Dorothy is in the center of the tray, behind the castle. In the tray, it appears that the journey will take her towards the fearful images of a large black spider, a bleeding skull, two monsters, a sinking man and a wounded man, and a dinosaur skeleton. John had entered therapy with a defensive and guarded attitude. His wife insisted upon his participation so that they could deepen in their relationship. Although he was willing, he was skeptical. After months of verbal therapy, he reluctantly began to work in the sand. He was astounded to notice the feelings and insight that arose with this approach. This tray marked the beginning of a deepening journey for him, where he acknowledged his fears and confusion, and began to express himself with increased authenticity and emotion. Both he and his wife were delighted with the intimacy that developed as his therapy progressed.

Sand Scene 7-2

This next scene (Sand Scene 7-2) was done by a 48-year-old woman who was neglected by her alcoholic mother and raised by an abusive grandmother. She was angry and depressed, and confused about why she felt this way. Although Marilyn's grandmother took care of her physical needs adequately, she often complained and expressed resentment over her situation. Marilyn was taught that the world is a frightening and harmful place, and that she must constantly be alert to danger. Marilyn grew up feeling guilty, insecure and unable to maneuver in her life successfully. Although she had demonstrated competence as a project manager and mother, internally she was filled with self-doubt and judgments of inadequacy. Although she was quite psychic and sensitive, traits she had inherited from her grandmother, she felt isolated and misunderstood as a result. *The Wizard of Oz* is a story she had strongly identified with since childhood. In her first sandtray scene, Dorothy is facing the Wicked Witch and other forces of darkness. Surprisingly, she had forgotten Dorothy's confrontation with the Wicked Witch until she created this picture. In this scene, there are two images of Dorothy, with a golden princess between them. They are successfully confronting the Wicked Witch and other forces of darkness that lay flattened in the sand. Glinda also lies flat on the sand, perhaps indicating that Marilyn must access her own resources and not rely on others to defeat the Wicked Witch. The ballerina that flanks her side may represent her growing independence from the strong maternal influences that have dominated her inner world.

In Sand Scene 7-3, done one week later, Marilyn celebrates her newfound freedom with Dorothy standing on a bridge between Jasmine and Glenda. She is surrounded with female heroines and idols, and seems to stand proudly in the midst of these powerful women. Following this tray, Marilyn was able to identify the destructive patterns and self-defeating beliefs that dominated her childhood. Just like Dorothy, Marilyn was able to leave the painful influences of her upbringing behind and discover her own internal power and identity.

Sand Scene 7-3

Sand Scene 7-4

In Sand Scene 7-4, Dorothy stands in the upper left corner of a tray filled with women heroines. Jennifer is a 65-year-old woman who found herself dazed and overwhelmed when her husband was diagnosed with a brain tumor. They had declared bankruptcy a year earlier, and were struggling financially as their productive working years were coming to an end. Although quite knowledgeable and psychologically sophisticated, Jennifer worked through her fears and insecurities with her images in the sand. Almost two years later, after descending into the depths of anxiety and confusion, she emerged to rebirth herself. This scene was done close to the completion of her therapy, and reveals her alignment with all women who have endured hardship and risen triumphantly. Dorothy is one of the many expressions of the feminine archetype found in this tray of victorious celebration.

Sand Scene 7-5

This next Sandplay scene (Sand Scene 7-5) was done by a sixty year old women who had been shattered by a traumatic experience at work. She was quite happy in her marriage, but as a result she lacked self-confidence in the workplace. She was very intuitive, and worked in a predominantly male environment where her sensitivities were not appreciated. We followed the guidance of her dreams, and identified the skills necessary to perform successfully at work. As she began to focus her attention and communicate more effectively, she was able to stay calm and non-reactive. Her self-confidence grew and she gained the respect of her co-workers that she thought she had lost. Towards the end of her therapy she completed this tray. At first she identified herself with Pooh, and described herself crouching in the corner under the trees. As she talked though, she began to identify with the fisherman, and to feel her attraction to the mysteries contained in the pyramid. Although she did not mention the figure of Dorothy, it is interesting that she placed it in such a predominate position. Dorothy is accompanied by her intuitive self embodied in Toto, and Glinda faces directly opposite providing support and encouragement. It seems "Dorothy" has acquired the strength now to delve more deeply into the mysteries contained in the pyramid, and that she is surrounded with the guidance and support necessary to undertake this adventure.

It is apparent from the ways Dorothy is used in Sandplay that people identify with her easily. She seems to represent the undeveloped and unsophisticated aspects of a person who realizes they need to expand their resources to face impending challenges. Her image seems to appear in a Sandplay process at significant and strategic times. Often she enters a Sandplay scene at the beginning of a person's journey into psychological healing. There is a hopeful quality with her presence, and often images of rainbows and protective powers give hope for a successful outcome. As a person continues with their therapy, Dorothy may appear later with skills to confront dark, scary, and witch-like situations. Finally, when the difficulties have been overcome and the resources within a person have been strengthened, Dorothy becomes a representation of inner wholeness or returning home. Her presence then reflects an integrated ego that can survive in the world, and revels an experience of wholeness that comes from self-recognition and relaxation into being home.

GLINDA

The Good Witch often appears in a Sandplay to signify protection or safety. Perhaps she is used to represent the therapist, who provides a sanctuary for inner exploration and healing. In Sand Scene 7-6, a 38-year-old woman creates a scene where she is deepening into the inner recesses of her psyche. She finds nourishment there with the Pepsi glass, but also find a disembodied hand and a clump of moss. Glinda stands at the edge of this damp hole, across from an angel. They seem to be holding a space for her inner work to progress. Naomi had recently separated from her husband and although she was able to support herself as an accountant, she was dissatisfied with her job and eager to return to school. She was in the process of stripping away the masks she had hidden behind during her marriage, and examining what lay beneath them. Although she was quite anxious about what she might find, she was also excited to get to know herself free from the confines of a defined relationship. When she made this scene, she had been feeling quite depressed and fearful; however, seeing the state of her inner world reflected in the sand seemed to life her spirits. She moved quickly through her confusion and anxiety, and within a year had enrolled in a masters degree program to peruse her dreams.

Sand Scene 7-6

In this scene (Figure 7-7) Glinda is surrounded with 3 rabbits and a dancing girl, and seems to be in direct confrontation with a number of demons and monsters. The image was created by a 36-year-old woman who was raised in a very religious home that stressed being good to avoid punishment. Dancing and other forms of self-expression were not allowed.

Here she uses Glinda for protection so that she can relax and follow her natural inclination to move her body. However, the naked woman in the center of the tray seems to be hidings her eyes in shame. It appears that forces of good and evil are battling within her, and that resolve the tensions within to find the way home.

Sand Scene 7-7

THE SCARECROW

In Sand Scene 7-8, after many months of verbal therapy, a 45-year-old woman began her Sandplay scenes with this image. The Scarecrow is the predominate figure in the tray, and he is facing a mirror. It seems she is eager to find the wisdom she knows is hidden within herself. The therapy unfolded as she peeled back layers of conditioning and inhibitions that had prevented her from appreciating and expressing herself. Throughout this time she often appeared confused and without direction, but she examined her experiences ruthlessly, and like the Scarecrow began to appreciate the patterns and lessons that life contained. Her persistence and determination finally led her into a state of inner peace and clarity, and she is now able to handle life's frustrations without becoming overwhelmed.

Sand Scene 7-8

Sand Scene 7-9

In the next scene (Sand Scene 7-9), a 35-year-old woman lays out the parameters of her journey at the beginning of a therapy process. There is a rainbow like archway at one end, and an Indian mystic at the other. Along the path are the Scarecrow, the Wicked

Witch, a wise man, an angel, a big dog, a singing smurf, a Rasta man and a suffering yogi. It seems she is describing the areas she will be exploring in the next few months of therapy. I could see from her image of the Scarecrow that it was important for her to understand her self and her journey, and that this would be a crucial part of finding her way home.

THE TIN WOODMAN

In Sand Scene 7-10 the Tin Woodman is beginning a journey towards Dorothy, where he hopes to reconnect with his heart and heal his internal wounds. He has a variety of obstacles to overcome before arriving at his destination though. The scene was created by a 34-year-old man whose alcoholic father disappeared when he was young leaving him to care for his grieving and dysfunctional mother, and physically disabled brother. His childhood was interrupted dramatically as he stepped into the shoes of his father's responsibility. As an adult George partnered with a single mother with two small children, and resentfully struggled as an artist to support his newfound family. In this sand scene, he blatantly displays his wounded heart and his hopes for healing that he imagines will come in the presence of the feminine as represented by Dorothy.

Sand Scene 7-10

THE COWARDLY LION

In this Sandplay session (Sand Scene 7-11), a young woman in the midst of a career change filled her scene with images of cats and lions. She had been a successful professional, but was unhappy in her corporate position where she was surrounded with competitive men. Although she had been offered lucrative advancements, she realized she was needed a change. She stopped working, entered therapy, and began an intense program of personal growth. Without the secure structure of a work schedule, she began to question everything, and slipped into a state of confusion and despair. Sandplays during this time were empty and vacant, with little movement or indication of life. The tray of the cats and lions was one of the first to reveal the inner strength and self-confidence that was building within her. She described in detail the admirable traits of cats and lions, and how important these animals had been to her throughout her life. It seemed to me she was beginning to access the courage and life force needed for the soul journey she had undertaken. Months later, after identifying and separating from the prison of her family's expectations, she began to explore art and photography, and embraced a lifestyle that included these channels of creativity. Expressing herself through art gave her a vehicle for tapping into her unconscious directly, and she rebuilt her life successfully with a resulting sense of wholeness. Today she functions as a competent entrepreneur and professional businesswoman.

Sand Scene 7-11

THE WIZARD

In Sand Scene 7-12 scene a 47-year-old man placed the things he did not want to see behind a screen. His father had recently died, and rather than surrender to the grieving process, he frantically filled his time with activities. When he created this picture in the sand, he realized how he was attempting to avoid his feelings around the loss of his father. Like the Wizard, he was creating a façade to hide behind, and now could see the futility of his efforts. He began to address these uncomfortable feelings in his therapy, and was able to move forward in his life without restriction.

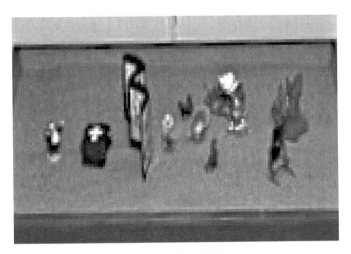

Sand Scene 7-12

SILVER SLIPPERS

Sand Scene 7-13 shows a scene made by a 54-year-old woman who was just emerging from a severe depression. Barren and lifeless sand scenes were replaced with lush greenery as she began to feel the joy of living once again. Although she is still struggling emotionally, in this tray she placed Dorothy's silver shoes. It seems she has found the means to return home to herself, and now is ready to learn how to do that. She continued to work diligently in her therapy, and the remnants of her depression dissolved as she entered into a new relationship and found her way into a satisfying work situation.

Sand Scene 7-13

Through the metaphors of Oz, a language of images has emerged that allows people to express the hopes, struggles, and rewards of the journey home. Dorothy and her friends seem to have arisen from the depths of the collective unconscious to give concrete form to the process of self-discovery and the awakening of consciousness. Although the story was written primarily for entertainment, it touches the depths of each soul's longing for peace and happiness. It is obvious from these examples what a powerful vehicle it has become, and how accurately it portrays the confusing issues that surround personal growth and development.

Pathway of Awakening

Chapter Eight
The Yellow Brick Road of Life

You must walk. It is a long journey, through a country that is sometimes pleasant and sometimes dark and terrible.
L. Frank Baum, *The Wonderful Wizard of Oz*, Chapter II

The path to the Emerald City is paved with yellow bricks. It is not always an easy path to follow, but its color is so bright it can be readily recognized. The Yellow Brick Road reminds me of the color of the sun. In a bath of yellow sunlight, nothing is hidden. Even shadows disappear when the sun is at the apex of its journey across the sky. Symbolically, this ball of fire is associated with the light of conscious awareness.

When Dorothy begins her journey in Oz she expects this golden path of bricks to lead her home. With the help of the Wizard, her desire seems simple and easy to accomplish. She has no idea about the complexity of her wish and the difficulties she will face to achieve her goal. With naïveté and innocence she enthusiastically begins to walk along the yellow bricks. This is a road of consciousness though, and the attainment of her desires is not at the end of her journey. It is the adventure itself that will satisfy her heart's desire.

In eastern mythology, mystics describe a coiled yellow snake that lies at the base of the spine as Kundalini energy. It represents a potential power that releases and travels up the spinal column when an individual attains enlightenment. Just as this golden snake penetrates the unconscious regions of the psyche, the Yellow Brick Road's twisting curves pass through dark and confusing situations to lead Dorothy and her friend's home. When the journey is complete, they relax in a state of wholeness, contentment, and loving recognition of their true nature. Like a labyrinth that twists and turns in opposite directions until it reaches the center core, the Yellow Brick Road leads us home if we just continue moving forward along its path.

Dorothy actually takes three separate journeys while she is in the Land of Oz. Her first trip is from the East where her house lands, to the Emerald City in the center of this magical kingdom. Along the way she befriends the Scarecrow, the Tin Woodman, and the Cowardly Lion who help her reach the Wizard. Then Dorothy and her friends take a second journey into the yellow land of the West that has been darkened with the Witch's presence. Here they are captured, and forced to confront the powers of evil. Dorothy's last journey comes after the Wizard flies off in his balloon. She goes to Glinda's castle in the South where she discovers how to return to the ordinary reality of her home in Kansas.

When marked on a map of Oz, these three trips form an inverted triangle with the point facing south. In Tibetan culture, the chakra centers in the body are represented by geometrical forms. A triangle is the symbol for the heart chakra and generally rests with the point facing up. When the heart suffers emotional pain though, the triangle is inverted to signify the direction energy must move for healing to occur. Instinctual energy, passion, sexuality, power, and confidence all reside in the lower charkas. According to this system, Dorothy needs to access and integrate these energies to relieve her pain and fulfill her desires.

Examining the direction of her travels within the sacred circle further emphasizes the significance of Dorothy's journey. Her house lands in the East, the direction of the rising sun or enlightenment. She enters the strange and magical Land of Oz in the direction of consciousness and ceremonial beginnings. Then she travels to the heart of Oz where she encounters the disturbing lessons of the Wizard. He sends her to the West, into the land of the setting sun where she faces the most difficult task of the journey. She frees the Winkies from the oppressive domination of the Wicked Witch and returns to the center of Oz transformed. In her third journey Dorothy goes towards the South where the mid-day sun shines unencumbered. This is the direction of innocence, openness, and conscious awareness. Here Glinda points out the power of the Silver Slippers, and with this awareness Dorothy returns home. The protection of the good Witch of the North influences Dorothy's entire journey. Wisdom resides in the northern region, and through the Good Witch of the North's help, Dorothy's wisdom increases as her experiences in Oz accumulate.

THE SIGNIFICANCE OF COLORS IN OZ

Oz is a bountiful land of brilliant colors. They stimulate the imagination and create a climate of playful receptivity. Each color of the rainbow carries with it specific vibrations that trigger different emotions and reactions. The land of the Munchkins where Dorothy arrives is colored blue. On the rainbow arc blue is close to the earth, and is associated with feelings of expansion, calmness, and healing. It is the color of the throat chakra, which represents communication and language.

One of Dorothy's unique characteristics is her inclination to communicate. When she arrives in Oz she speaks openly to the Good Witch of the North and immediately requests help and guidance. Dorothy speaks with and befriends the man stuffed with straw, and later the man made of tin. She chastises the Cowardly Lion when he attacks Toto, confronts the Wizard when he fails to keep his promise, and tries to negotiate with the Wicked Witch while being held prisoner in her castle. Dorothy's arrival in the blue land of the Munchkins emphasizes how important communication is for the successful completion of her journey as a feminine heroine.

Dorothy then travels to the Emerald city where she is required to wear green glasses. The Emerald City is surrounded by primary colors and lies directly between blue and yellow, the colors of the East and West. It holds a central position in Oz, and comes from the blending of these two basic colors. Green is farther from the earth, follows blue in the rainbow's arc, and is a color of vibrancy and growth. It paints the lush vegetation and abundant foliage of Mother Earth and creates an atmosphere of growth, balance, relaxation, and love. Emeralds are the brilliant green gems associated with rain, fertility, immortality, and hope. Alchemists value the emerald's ability to stimulate the expression of reason, dexterity, and wisdom.

According to Baum, people are required to don green glasses before entering the Emerald City so their eyes are not damaged by the brilliance of its sparkling gems. Instead of rose-colored glasses, the Emerald City radiates the color of the heart chakra and requires all who enter to embrace its magic.

The Yellow Brick Road guides Dorothy through the colorful Land of Oz. Yellow follows green in the rainbow arc, and is associated with the solar plexus. This is the energy center of the body that represents personal power, clear thinking, and learning. Dorothy must travel the road of yellow bricks and confront the shadowy world of the Wicked Witch to access her power. The Winkies have been suppressed by the darkness of the Wicked Witch, but Dorothy's actions bring the light of freedom back into their land.

Because yellow resembles gold it generates thoughts of wealth, abundance, and material success. Gold is valued as a precious metal and treasured by many cultures. For centuries alchemists patiently and unabashedly attempted to create it from various raw materials. Their process for transforming metals has become a concrete expression for understanding the complexities of life itself. Just like Dorothy, following the path of gold led them into a discovery of life's most profound truths.

In her third journey, Dorothy goes into the red territory of Glinda, the Good Witch of the South, who resides over the Quadlings who live there. Red is the color of the root chakra where the powerful energies of survival and passion reside. It is here that the Kundalini lies coiled and waiting to awaken. According to ancient healing systems, activating the energy of the root chakra leads to transformation. Red is the closest to the heavens in the rainbow arc.

When all the colors of this magical bow have been traversed, myths of the rainbow suggest that a bridge is created allowing access to the heavenly realms. In alignment with this imagery, Dorothy is able to return home only after she has traveled to Glinda's castle in the red territory of the south.

CHALLENGES OF THE JOURNEY

The central theme of most great fairy tales is the struggle to accomplish noble deeds by overcoming formidable obstacles. The Oz story is no exception. The first problem Dorothy encounters as she travels to the Emerald City is crossing a deep ravine. It is so wide that it seems impassible. Dorothy has no idea how to proceed. It is the Scarecrow who solves the dilemma, telling the Cowardly Lion to leap across the abyss with the travelers on his back. The success of this bold action begins to give the Cowardly Lion the courage and confidence he so desperately desires.

Every journey begins with a leap into the unknown. Although it can be frightening, when people courageously jump into the abyss of the unknown, they must intuitively trust they will be shown the way. Their familiarity with the past must be left behind so the new adventure can be embraced without encumbrances. After passing through the initial anxieties that come with all new beginnings, a surge of excitement and confidence often follows.

As the three travelers continue along the Yellow Brick Road, they encounter ferocious Kalidahs. With the bodies of tigers and the heads of bears, these beasts are both savage and uncontrollable. To protect Dorothy and her friends, the Cowardly Lion lets out a tremendous roar that frightens the creatures, but this is just a momentary solution. The travelers continue to be pursued until they come to a bottomless gorge. The Scarecrow hurriedly suggests that the Tin Woodman create a bridge with a tree trunk, and they dart across just seconds before the bridge collapses and the Kalidahs tumble to their death. Again, Dorothy is saved by the ingenuity of her companions.

When venturing into new territory, we often fear attack, destruction, or even death. In the psyche's dream world, these fears sometimes take the form of wild animals or imaginary monsters. They challenge us to confront and conquer our fears, and to act courageously when we are most terrified. As Dorothy demonstrates so vividly, these terrors must be overcome to continue our journey.

The next hurdle the travelers face is crossing a raging river. It flows over the Yellow Brick Road and prevents them from moving forward. The Scarecrow and Tin Woodman build a raft to cross the water, but they lose control of it in the fast flowing current. The Scarecrow is left clinging to a pole in the middle of the river, and Dorothy, Toto, the Cowardly Lion, and the Tin Woodman are carried downstream. The Cowardly Lion then courageously swims the raft to shore so the three companions can continue their journey. They are far from the Yellow Brick Road though, and saddened to loose their straw-filled friend. Surprisingly, they meet a stork on the riverbank who offers to rescue the Scarecrow. Just like a newborn baby, he is delivered to his friends and they resume their travels together.

The Scarecrow's mishap is a reminder of how quickly strong emotions can flood our inner world and immobilize us with confusion and indecision. The liquid fluidity of flowing water resembles the ebb and flow of strong emotions that can rage through our bodies when we are upset. Just as the Scarecrow is saved after re-establishing contact with Dorothy and her companions, so too are we calmed and nourished in the presence of loving friends. The Scarecrow's rescue implies that mobility, balance, and centeredness can be regained, not only by being with friends, but also by connecting with forgotten parts of our self.

Following this event, the travelers are eager to reach the Emerald City. They decide to take a short cut through a Poppyfield. The fragrance of the deadly flowers puts Dorothy, Toto, and the Cowardly Lion into a deep sleep. The Scarecrow and Tin Woodman carry Dorothy and Toto out of the intoxicating field, but the Cowardly Lion is too big to move. When the Tin Woodman saves the Queen of the Field Mice from being devoured by a wildcat, her subjects offer to help. The Scarecrow again conceives of a plan, and the mice band together to rescue the king of the jungle.

So often we approach the completion of a project accompanied by feelings of lethargy and resistance. There just doesn't seem to be enough energy to finish the task. For example, think about the times you have started a creative project. You conceive an idea and get the materials together, beginning it with great enthusiasm. As the work continues though there often arises a great reluctance to complete it, especially if it is not turning out the way you had imagined. As anxiety about a project builds, it is easy to slip into a state of procrastination and indecisiveness that numbs us like the fragrant field of poppies. Drugs, alcohol, and other addictive behaviors help us to avoid these uncomfortable feelings. Procrastination, resistance, and addictions are deadly poisons that sap our energy and prevent us from mobilizing our resources. The fragrant Poppyfield is a grave reminder of how we can become immobilized in this journey. Like being paralyzed within the invisible tendrils of an unconscious web, it would be easy to slip away from our goals in a sleepy daze, and wander aimlessly without focus or motivation. Like any intoxicant, the Poppyfield seduces the travelers just before their arrival at the Emerald City. It is only with the help of the Scarecrow's intelligence, the Tin Woodman's compassion, and the Field Mice's instinctual energy that Dorothy and her companions awaken to complete their journey.

After their visit with the Wizard, the travelers are surprised to discover there is no Yellow Brick Road into the West. It is not a popular place to visit. They follow the setting sun, and as they approach the Wicked Witch's castle she send her armies out to destroy them. The Scarecrow stops a flock of fighting crows by defiantly wringing each of their necks. The Tin Woodman beheads a pack of ferocious wolves before they cause any harm, and together the Scarecrow and Tin Woodman defeat a swarm of killer bees. The Scarecrow protects Dorothy, Toto, and the Lion by covering them with his straw, and the bees break their stingers on the Tin Woodman, dying at his feet. Finally, in desperation, the Wicked Witch sends the Winged Monkeys to destroy the Scarecrow and Tin Woodman, and bring Dorothy, Toto, and the Cowardly Lion back to her castle.

When traveling into the dark regions of the psyche, we often feel overwhelmed by the destructive forces encountered there. Courage, wisdom, and compassion must each be activated to overcome these negative energies. Even when times are darkest, just like Dorothy and her friends we must stand up against attack and hold firm to our resolve. This is not an easy task. It requires us to draw on the depths of our resources and maintain a focused and disciplined attitude so that we can move successfully through these tunnels of darkness and despair.

The Flying Monkeys are strange anomalies. They live on Mother Earth as mammals who embody instinctual energy, and they have wings that catapult them into Father Sky where they fly unencumbered by the limitations of gravity. Although they appear to have great powers, the Flying Monkeys must do the bidding of their owner. As servants of the Wicked Witch, they are destructive emissaries of evil. When Dorothy obtains possession of the Witch's Magic Cap though, they instantly surrender to her. Instinctual energy can be used for good or evil. When the forces of darkness govern, it becomes violent and destructive; when used with the light of awareness, it fosters higher consciousness.

Difficulties and hardships continue when Dorothy embarks on her third journey to the south. Trees try to pull the travelers into the frightening recesses of a forbidden forest, and a giant spider tries to trap them there. The Scarecrow and Tin Woodman again combine their skills to outwit the grasping trees, and the Cowardly Lion courageously kills the monstrous arachnid. They successfully resist the dangers of a forest that could destroy them with its untamed energy.

As they continue towards Glinda's castle the travelers must cultivate sensitivity, awareness, and mindfulness to pass through a land of breakable china without hurting anyone. Here we learn to become aware of how our actions affect others. People who avoid the challenges of life become fragile and brittle, like these china figurines. They isolate themselves to prevent being injured, making it difficult for others to maneuver among them. In Baum's story, only the church is shattered accidentally by the Cowardly Lion, perhaps indicating its vulnerability in the presence of the Lion's strong instinctual energy.

Finally the travelers face the Hammerheads whole hardheaded attacks stop them from going any further. Like the stubbornness of old thought patterns, their heads pound the travelers relentlessly, preventing them from going on. They call on the instinctual energy of the Flying Monkeys to deliver them to Glinda. Although they once served the Wicked Witch, with Dorothy as their master they respond to her wishes without hesitation.

In any journey, obstacles and problems appear. By finding the means to overcome difficulties, wisdom, compassion, courage, and awareness emerge. Dorothy's enthusiasm and determination motivate the Scarecrow, the Tin Woodman, and the Cowardly Lion to seek their heart's desire, but they would not have attained their goals without each other's help. How easy it is to be defeated by unexpected challenges! Treacherous gorges, ravenous monsters, and fast flowing rivers expose each character's fears and insecurities. The Poppyfield, the Witch's armies, and the terrors of the Forest of Fighting Trees force them to use untapped skills and reserves. The land of China develops sensitivity and attentiveness, and the impassable Hammerheads force them to bypass the stubbornness of old beliefs and mindsets. Only when all these hardships have been overcome is Dorothy ready for the transformation that will take her home. Success demands nothing less than risking one's life and totally surrendering to the challenges of the moment in order to reach the final state of self-realization.

Year ago, when I was beginning to teach about *The Wizard of Oz*, a friend began to paint a large Yellow Brick Road on butcher paper, to be used as a creative decoration. With great enthusiasm she showed Dorothy arriving in the colorful Land of Oz, and setting off on her journey across cornfields and through forests. When the road stopped at the edge of a bottomless pit, she sank into a lethargic state and could not continue with her project. We directly discussed the possible implications of this, and without further consideration moved forward with our lives. A few years later, after she had been through a difficult divorce and restructuring of her life, we remembered the bottomless pit and her inability to complete the art project. As we looked back, it appeared she had to figure a way to cross her own bottomless pit before she could finish the Yellow Brick Road and continue forward with her life.

Chapter Nine
Witches and Wizards

You must keep my secret and tell no one I am a humbug.
L. Frank Baum, *The Wonderful Wizard of Oz,* Chapter XV

After successfully overcoming their first series of obstacles, Dorothy and her companions dance with excitement at the thought of obtaining their hearts' desires. They eagerly knock on the great doors of the Emerald City, and although treated graciously, are surprised they must wear green spectacles to enter the city. The true nature of Oz is disguised, perhaps with the unspoken hopes and expectations of its inhabitants.

The revered Wizard lives in a magnificent castle that insulates him from people and encourages an innocent belief in his magical powers. Although he successfully maintains a majestic illusion of authority, his changing form and illusive character hint at deception. Later, Toto's instinctive inquisitiveness exposes the Wizard's deceitful behavior.

The attempts of this ordinary man to control his environment reveal a familiar and self-defeating pattern often used to obtain security and stability. Think about the times we exaggerate the truth to make ourselves look good in another person's eyes, or the times we try to impress others with our expertise or experience in an area we know little about. Like the Wizard we attempt to create an image of authority or power, when in truth we are just hiding behind a screen of illusion. We deceive ourselves into believing that our insecurities and inadequacies are well hidden, and must maintain this façade with great attentiveness in order to sustain our deception. Eventually life uncovers these masks though, and like the Wizard we must acknowledge the humbug within who is afraid to be seen.

When Dorothy and her friends arrive at the Emerald City after melting the Wicked Witch, they are shocked to discover the Wizard is really a balloonist from Nebraska. After Dorothy chastises him, he carefully shows the Scarecrow, the Tin Woodman, and the Cowardly Lion that they already possess the qualities they desire. He also promises to help Dorothy by preparing his balloon for a return flight to America. With his image of power having been shattered though, his response to Dorothy and her friends is that of an ordinary man willing to help her friends. At this point, because of his trickery it is tempting to dismiss the importance of the Wizard's contribution to the story. He acts as a trickster, in the language of archetypes, by enticing Dorothy and her friends into a threatening situation that serves to develop and strengthen each of them. In his role as trickster he is a great teacher, and when he is uncovered as a humbug he reflects to each of the characters what they had been unable to see in themselves. Then in a sprit of loving generosity, the beauty of his heart is revealed with his simple offer to help Dorothy and identify the inner qualities of her friends.

The Wizard's behavior is a reminder of the shimmering veils of illusion we often use to protect our vulnerability and hide our fears and insecurities. We see in him the false bravado of an inflated ego attempting to conceal the machinations of a mind spinning out of control. It is not until the curtains of self-deception are pulled away though, that we are able to respond authentically and compassionately to the needs of others.

So often when people come into my office, they are hiding behind a curtain like the Wizard, afraid to let themselves be seen. I am reminded of a young man who often interrupted his therapy session with me to answer his cell phone and conduct business. He was in the process of a divorce, drinking heavily, wanting custody of his children, trying to establish a new relationship, and unwilling to step away from his role as budding entrepreneur long enough to address the confusion of his personal life. Although he imagined himself to be competent and successful, his pretentious façade of activity and addiction was growing thin. Like the Wizard he seemed to be frantically calling out, "Pay no attention to that man behind the screen." His family and friends watched helplessly as his life spun out of control. It was not until his business failed, his girlfriend left, and his children were placed in the custody of their mother that he began to acknowledge his own internal pain and relax into self-acceptance. With this came the relief and freedom of being himself without having to maintain the pressures of self-deception and false images.

Most of us cling tightly to the unfounded belief that we can control the events in our lives. When we find this is not possible, as indeed we will, we look for guidance about how to overcome our perceived shortcomings and improve our performance. Advertisements inundate us with fantasies of quick solutions and magical potions, and we willingly sacrifice money, time, and energy to follow promises of mastery, satisfaction, and fulfillment. The truth is though, that we are not as powerful as we would like to believe. The thoughts we think, the emotions we feel, and even the next breath we take cannot be regulated or controlled. Our vision, like Dorothy's, has been clouded by spectacles of delusion. Before we can return home we must remove these lenses of misguided beliefs, and dissolve our fantasy that an all-knowing Wizard can somehow manipulate the environment to give us what we want.

THE WIZARD'S TEST

In most stories of a heroic journey, the Wizard acts as a guardian and representative for all that is known. He stands as a sentinel marking the boundary into unknown territory. Although reaching this Wizard is expected to be the end of the journey, it is actually the beginning of a more profound experience. Joseph Campbell calls the ultimate challenge of the Wizard the "Wizard's Test." It must be successfully completed to transcend ordinary reality and attain the real treasure of the quest. The Wizard, like the one who lives in Oz, acts as a trickster to entice the hero or heroine to continue their journey. Without the trickery of the Wizard, the climax of the heroic quest could easily be missed. It is not a situation one enters eagerly.

Often we are motivated to begin a project by envisioning its final outcome. Like looking down a country road, we expect our dreams to materialize just beyond the first curve. Thoughts of success pull us forward, but as the road twists and curves our fears can paralyze us with inertia. Although Dorothy and her friends expect to fulfill their desires when they first meet the Wizard, as with any transformative venture, they must courageously continue beyond the Wizard's domain into frightening, unfamiliar, and foreign territory. Success comes only when the road is followed to its completion, regardless of the fears, frustrations, and disappointments that might arise.

When I was teaching, I saw many graduate students began their study of Clinical Psychology with great enthusiasm and excitement. They imagined themselves as successful psychotherapists, and were eager to complete the training that would prepare them for this. Academic study is just the beginning of this path, though. As they delved deeper into the inner world of psychological functioning, their own demons had to be confronted, and their inner wounds healed. The challenges of academic tests, professional internships, and licensing exams are compounded with the personal crises that often erupt during a student's professional development. "Physician heal you" is a powerful training ground for the person who desires to work in this field, and the struggles of entering into the dark and foreign territory of the unknown must be overcome in order to become a competent psychotherapist. There is no way to predict the difficulties that will arise before a journey begins, and each one of these challenges must be successfully overcome to develop the skills necessary for facilitating emotional healing.

The Wizard shakes Dorothy's hope of returning to Kansas with his request for her to obtain the Wicked Witch's broomstick.

Although he promises to help, the Wizard's Test is most abhorrent to Dorothy. She thinks of herself as a good girl who is kind to others and does what she is told. Now she must relinquish this self-image for another. Although she does not realize all this when she accepts the Wizard's Test, she most likely feels the inner conflict that this venture creates. She must now open her own dark side to release repressed aggression and anger and slay dragons of fear and insecurity. This is what is needed to return home.

Attaining a healthy and confident attitude requires a person to become aware of the undesirable qualities that lurk in the shadow lands of their psyche. Although we would like to eliminate these dark and disturbing qualities, they live surreptitiously behind images of social conformity, and erupt uncontrollably when defenses weaken. In order for consciousness to develop, they must be identified and accepted as an integral part of one's self. Although it is difficult and unsettling to examine these hidden traits, if they remain unexplored, a cardboard person emerges void of spontaneity, intuition, and emotional expressiveness. Like a seed that absorbs the refuge of a garden to grow and blossom, exploration of the dark, discarded material of the psyche releases a tremendous energy that activates untapped potentials and stimulates unexpected growth. When this shadow material is brought to light, it fuels the expression of creativity, vitality, passion, and sensitivity, providing fertile ground for the expression of a rich and multi-faceted personality.

ACCESSING THE SHADOW SELF

In *The Wonderful Wizard of Oz*, Dorothy's journey leads to an inevitable confrontation with the Wicked Witch. This is a dark energy, and represents a part of ourselves that we deny and repress into unconsciousness. In Jungian terms this is called the "shadow," or shadow material. It is the part of us that we do not like and pretend does not exist. When confronted with its presence through our own actions or another's feedback, we often respond with vehement denial or intense defensiveness. For example, if we think of ourselves as generous and kind, and then are accused of being stingy or mean, we will typically deny the accusation and respond with anger or irritation.

Frequently shadow material is projected onto others, and then criticized or rejected as undesirable. When we describe the characteristics of another person, we are often describing aspects of ourselves that we are unwilling to accept for one reason or another. Most often we see the parts of ourselves we dislike and criticize, but surprisingly we also see the desirable and powerful parts of ourselves that we are afraid to accept or integrate. Although we are often blind to this behavior, great strides in our personal growth occur when we acknowledge our judgments of others as expressions of ourselves. Blind spots, by definition are invisible, and recognizing our own shadow material is the most challenging. It destroys the illusion of who we imagine ourselves to be and brings into awareness aspects of ourselves that are uncomfortable.

Even though the Wicked Witch epitomizes negativity, selfishness, destruction, and evil, when captured by the despicable woman, Dorothy attempts to please her. She believes that if she is good enough, she will be treated fairly. This is a survival technique familiar to many of us, and acquired in response to situations from early childhood. It does not always get us what we want and need though. When the Witch trips the innocent heroine with an invisible bar, Dorothy's composure dissolves and she defiantly hurls a pail of water at the wicked woman, tapping into an inner wellspring of anger, outrage, and ferocious self-defense. These are aspects of Dorothy's shadow, well hidden with her outward appearance of goodness and compliance. Although it is upsetting for someone like Dorothy to uncover these seemingly undesirable traits, it is essential for her well being to access these energies. Once they have been exposed, like the instinctual energy represented by the Flying Monkeys, they can be used in the service of higher consciousness.

Shedding light onto shadow material is usually disturbing and challenging. However, eliminating negative traits by repressing them into the unconscious only results in their persistent appearance in reactive behavior patterns. The inner world then acts as a battle-ground between what is acceptable and unacceptable, creating an internal division between the conflicting parts of the self. It is only when the shadow is encompassed by the light of consciousness that it is transformed into positive energy.

We repress undesirable traits because they create conflict and discomfort. Accepting the uncomfortable aspects of ourselves requires an innovative reorganization of the psyche. This happens when hidden characteristics are brought into consciousness, accepted, and integrated as part of a healthy self-concept. When this occurs, not only are the undesirable traits exposed, but also valuable energy that was inadvertently bound with them is released. Dorothy had to directly confront and melt the Wicked Witch to tap into these energies and continue her development.

If I look at my own experiences, I remember when it was difficult for me to disagree with someone. I wanted to be loved and accepted, and saw myself as irritating, obnoxious, and insensitive when I expressed my own opinions. I labeled my own thoughts as selfish, dark, and unacceptable, and tried to eliminate them. I strove to be supportive, loving, and understanding of others at all times, but often felt invisible, oppressed, and unable to relax and enjoy life. As I attempted to identify the source of my inner disturbance, I remember that as a child I was discouraged from expressing myself. Attempts to communicate or disagree with my parents were seen as defiance, and I learned early in life to adopt a defensive attitude of outward compliance.

Although I valiantly attempted to maintain this image, I was unable to control the temper outbursts that emerged when things did not go my way. These reactions stimulated critical self-judgments, and an internal battle began to rage with my anger and compliance battling each other for control. I adopted an arrogant attitude of self-righteous, and pushed my negative self-criticisms into the shadows of my unconscious. As I engaged in a path of consciousness and began to explore internal conflicts, I became aware that I was labeling any expression of my personal needs or opinions as selfish. This recognition was one of the first steps towards successfully dissolving the temper outbursts and eventually led me to identifying my needs without embarrassment. I began to focus on how to communicate, learning to tolerate uncomfortable feelings so that I could complete a conversation. I found that unlocking the doors shadow lands like this is essential for the development of self-expression and healthy relationships.

In the Oz story, Dorothy grabs for a pail of water when she gets angry. With the magic of all serendipitous moments, she has reached for one of the few things that terrifies the Wicked Witch. During the time of the inquisition, many women were drowned to test their innocence or guilt as witches. There was no way out of the "water test." If they survived the drowning, they were judged guilty and burned; if they died, they were considered innocent but lost their lives in the process. It is ironic that the Wicked Witch of the West's final demise comes from exposure to water. Water is the powerful media from which all living things emerge. It is used in ritual to signify the purification and cleansing of body, mind, emotion, and spirit, and is a universal symbol of fertility. The "water of life" used for baptism is believed to be more effective than any prayer or mantra for protection against enemies, catastrophes, and evil spirits. It symbolizes a return to our original state and carries the manifestation of new life and creative possibilities. It is with the assistance of this powerful medium that Dorothy cleanses her spirit, dissolves her inhibitions, and purifies her psyche. In this moment of liberation, the old image she had of herself dies and she is reborn through the waters of life, into the wholeness of her self.

GOOD AND EVIL PERSONIFIED

As is typical of shadow material, the Wicked Witch of the West appears as soon as Dorothy ventures into her territory. Often when we open the door to our inner world, we suffer with uncomfortable feelings and disturbing insights. Initially we strengthen our defenses and battle these demons, just like the three travelers when they destroy the Wicked Witch's wolves, crows, and bees. In the story though, Dorothy, Toto, and the Cowardly Lion are eventually overpowered and carried as prisoners to the Wicked Witch's forbidding castle. When defenses crumble in the face of adversity, it is easy to become engulfed by dark and confusing feelings. The Witch's castle shows us this quite dramatically. Even in this seemingly hopeless situation though, Dorothy sneaks food to the Cowardly Lion who is isolated in the basement. Nurturing the instinctive energy of the Lion at this time sustains and strengthens her own vitality, and Dorothy shows us again the strength of her indomitable spirit. It is this attitude that will lead her out of imprisonment. Later, when she obtains mastery over the Flying Monkeys and frees the Cowardly Lion, this energy is available for her confrontation with the Wizard and her journey south to see Glinda.

Although most of us are quite familiar with evil witches, in Oz we are reminded that witches can also be good. Dorothy herself is acclaimed as a good and powerful sorceress, and is immediately seen as an enemy of evil when her house kills the Wicked Witch of the East. The Land of Oz is divided into four distinct quadrants, and witches rule each of them. Good witches govern territories in the north and south, and evil ones dominate the lands of the east and west. The evil witches fight for increased power, but are stopped by the good witches who maintain a delicate balance between the two forces. Dorothy's appearance as a personification of consciousness disrupts this stability and creates internal turmoil.

When Dorothy shatters the evil oppression of the Wicked Witch of the East, the Good Witch of the North instantly appears to support her. Dorothy is advised how to find the Wizard, and blessed with a kiss on the center of her forehead to protect her from harm. This spot is identified as the seat of the "third eye" or the chakra center of intuition and insight. Although the good witches cannot overpower the evil ones, they support Dorothy to bring a new dimension into their unresolved conflict between good and evil. Perhaps the kiss of the Good Witch is a reminder for Dorothy to follow her intuition, as well as a talisman to protect her from destruction.

Dorothy arrives in Oz as an innocent child, eager to please others and unaware of her own vulnerability. The Good Witch recognizes the purity of Dorothy's heart and willingly offers protection to safeguard her journey.

When I was divorced after a 12-year marriage, I felt like Dorothy, overwhelmed with feelings of confusion and imprisoned in a castle of darkness. I found myself questioning the very roots of my identity. Although I had explored the path of Christianity with great diligence as a child, it did not sustain me through my young adult years, and I turned towards the teachings of Buddhism and other eastern mystics for understanding and guidance. I wholeheartedly embraced a spiritual path and devoted myself to yoga and meditation to create an inner stability and balance that could not be shattered by external events. My spiritual guide at this time was a friend and mentor who believed in me and pointed me towards my own Yellow Brick Road. His presence reminds me of Glinda, gently blessing and guiding Dorothy at the beginning of her journey to find the way home. His unfailing acceptance provided a much needed sanctuary of support and strength. Just as Dorothy felt alone in the strange country of Oz, few people understood the tremendous upheaval I was experiencing internally. Acquaintances dropped away, friendships dissolved, and I found myself facing difficult situations without the support of familiar company.

I questioned all dogmas, and discarded any teachings that were not relevant to my inner experience. As I persisted in my quest for freedom, I was relieved to find the Four Noble Truths of the Buddha. Here was an acknowledgement of the suffering we all experience, as well as an understanding of the origins of unhappiness and a guideline for how to integrate these teachings into everyday life. He pointed towards a state of freedom where the mind could not engage in the complex phenomena of suffering, and showed how it would then dissolve and disappear. Through the teachings of the Buddha, I was able to see the universal truths that permeate all spiritual lessons, and like Dorothy I realized that integrating these messages into my life would carry me home. In Buddha's Eightfold Path

I saw how to live in harmony with the natural order of things, how to develop wisdom, compassion, and concentration, and how to see clearly through the veils of illusion that confuse and distort reality. His guidelines became a roadmap for me and I meticulously began to incorporate his teachings. Although his guidance appeared quite simple and straightforward, integrating the teachings into my life has become a life long endeavor. I have learned that satisfaction comes from living these principles in a mindful way, and that understanding, compassion and a sense of harmony with existence arise and expand as a result.

CHAPTER TEN
THERE'S NO PLACE LIKE HOME

Dorothy lived in the midst of the great Kansas prairies, with Uncle Henry who was a farmer, and Aunt Em who was the farmer's wife.
L. Frank Baum, *The Wonderful Wizard of Oz*, Chapter I

E ven the wildest adventurer treasures the simple delights of being in a loving home. It is here that harmony, peace, and communion with loved ones feeds the soul and opens the heart. Ideally home is a place where emotional and physical needs are easily met. It is a place of protection, security, relaxation, and unconditional acceptance. We let our guard down here, and find refuge from the confusing complexities of the outside world. Unfortunately, many people only dream about experiencing a loving home. Disappointments with life are often coupled with an insatiable desire for the shelter of this protective place.

Because technology has advanced at break neck speed creating a complex and challenging society, there is little time for relaxation or personal reflection. Although surrounded with a plethora of material goods and conveniences, personal energy and vitality are at a premium. Pushing to the point of exhaustion, people's bodies are breaking down with diseases like cancer, AIDS, and other auto-immune disorders. Addictive behaviors and psychological disturbances abound. There is hardly time to interact with loved ones, and the stress of earning a living and maintaining a household creates serious adults whose joy of living is replaced with blind attempts to survive. There are few models for coping with these catastrophic changes, and as a result, many people appear to be disconnected from the nurturing energy of their souls.

The road to inner peace and happiness is not paved with material possessions. Although America is one of the wealthiest countries in the world, unhappiness and discontent drive its citizens into competitive lifestyles that emphasize monetary success. Perhaps people are searching for something that has been lost in the rush of technological development, and have not yet looked in the places where it might be found.

Songs, films, and stories of all kinds remind us of the pleasures of home. Although Dorothy sings out at the beginning of the Oz movie about her longing to cross over the rainbow, it is her undaunted desire to return home that electrifies her story. Her journey is a reminder that the attainment of this cherished place is possible if we just follow the Yellow Brick Road. We need only find the path and resolutely face the obstacles that appear as we proceed.

At times we all experience feelings of strangeness and unfamiliarity about our existence on this planet. It is a cumbersome and confusing place where we repeatedly learn to live with the physical limitations of body and mind. The possibility of a place where these difficulties do not exist fills the heart with a deep yearning and hunger for fulfillment. In many spiritual traditions the satisfaction of this heartfelt desire is described as arriving in a heavenly domain of peace and happiness. Such a paradise is recognized in psychological language and the archetype "home."

EMBRACING ADVENTURE AND RETURNING HOME

Leaving home and relating to the outside world is an inevitability every child faces in the process of growing up. Toddlers naturally move away from the familiarity of mother to explore the world beyond their family. Although they may be hesitant at first to move out of mother's sight, their range of exploration expands as confidence increases. This is a normal process of development and essential for the flowering of an independent person. The return to mother is just as important as the urge to explore.

Although not as obvious, these cycles continue as we age. In life we move from the familiar to explore the unknown, and then back again to the familiar. If we examine the broader cycles of our lives, the ebb and flow of this pattern can be seen even in birth and death. Birth suggests an arrival, and a journey from somewhere else into this plane of existence. Death suggests a return to that place from which we emerged. For a child the place of origin and return is mother. For an adult, it is a spiritual abode we metaphorically call "home."

For Dorothy, the broad, gray, undifferentiated flatlands of Kansas represent not only her personal, but also her spiritual home. Kansas is reminiscent of the eternal source of oneness from which all beings emerge. Oz is much more than a fantasyland. It is a colorful manifestation of our experiences and activities on this planet, and provides a place for us to explore the richness of our being. Through our interactions and experiences on earth, we learn about our physical-spiritual-emotional nature, and finally come to realize that home resides in the invisible realm of our heart and soul. Some traditions call this physical plane the world of illusions, because it obscures the truth of who we really are. Oz is also a world of illusions and fantasies, where the truth of our being must be uncovered through personal experience.

Perhaps one of the reasons people are attracted strongly to *The Wonderful Wizard of Oz* is because it resonates with an experience of being strangers in a strange land. The story clarifies our situation, throws us into situations that resemble our own life experiences, and dramatically emphasizes the importance of home. Often we are anxious to leave our family for adventure, only to realize, once we are far away that we have left behind what we cherish most.

As a fantasy story, Oz appeals to people who want to escape life's frustrations and find solace in a world of make believe. People often tell me how Oz brings relief by creating a fantasy world where life's problems can be forgotten. For me though, Oz was never an escape.

Traveling into that enchanted kingdom just brought me closer to realizing my destiny. In the story it seems that Dorothy herself wants to escape Kansas. As the story unfolds though, we realize there is no escape for our heroine. Dorothy's difficulties follow her, and perhaps even intensify. For those who want to grow and develop, Dorothy's adventure provides a key for understanding who we are, what is important, and how to return home. For those who wish to escape, her story provides a temporary distraction from the mundane, and at the same time opens a doorway for living with a fresh perspective.

As a child I lived between the worlds of Oz and Kansas. I valued relating to others, and wanted to know everything I could about this physical plane. I was active, involved, and frustrated that I could not learn at a faster pace. The limitations of planet Earth reminded me of Dorothy's experience of Kansas, and her yearning for home resonated with my own yearning for a spiritual abode. As I began to explore the spiritual path though, I seemed to enter a dimension similar to Oz. Life became mysterious, unusual, and unfamiliar. I explored it as Dorothy explored Oz, eager to learn as much as I could, and realizing that my hunger for a spiritual home could only be satisfied by finding happiness wherever I happened to be.

As I have deepened in spiritual awareness, my life seems to resemble Dorothy's experiences in Oz more and more. Kansas has receded into the background, and I revel in the invisible world of spiritual awakening. The frustrations and limitations of life in Kansas have disappeared, and I find myself traveling form Kansas to Oz and back again effortlessly. Now it seems that Kansas and Oz are just different expressions of the same phenomena. In both these worlds we are challenged to awaken and realize the truth of who we are through our own experience.

Following the path of yellow bricks has awakened in me the understanding that "home is where the heart is." The world of matter and the world of spirit are different expressions of the same reality, and dancing between them creates a bridge of transcendence that encompasses both. Through living the journey of Dorothy, I have learned that life is filled with synchronistic surprises, apparent tragedies, and unexpected windfalls. Withdrawing from these experiences leaves a perception of the world that is as flat and barren as Dorothy's Kansas. Embracing the unexpected and pursuing serendipitous events awakens an awareness of the color and enchantment of life, as Dorothy experienced in the Land of Oz.

Finding home is a way to express the peace and contentment that arises when we are happy and relaxed wherever we are. While in the emptiness of Kansas, we simultaneously experience the richness of Oz, and in the dazzling beauty of Oz we recognize the presence of emptiness. There is no separation between Kansas and Oz. They are one, and as expressions of conscious awareness we live inside this paradoxical mystery. Awakening to this realization expands our concept of home to include the vastness of existence itself, and give space for gratitude, joy, wisdom, and compassion to arise naturally.

THE SPHERE OF WHOLENESS

Human beings are complex organisms whose physical form includes biological functions, thoughts, feelings, and sensory perceptions. We remember past experiences, imagine future possibilities, identify, calculate, classify, and organize information to create a sense of order and understanding. The horizontal plane on which we live broadens with awareness as we become more conscious of our psychological functioning and biological heritage.

Dorothy's encounters with the Scarecrow, the Tin Woodman, and the Cowardly Lion represent different ways we experience ourselves along this horizontal axis. They each need to be integrated into a conscious sense of self to accomplish the journey home. In metaphysical circles, wisdom, love, and power form the divine spark of a threefold flame that lives within the heart. When this flame is activated to its fullest potential, the highest form of enlightenment is attained. In the language of Oz, this enlightenment is represented by Dorothy's arrival home.

Most of us experience difficulties in our expression of wisdom, love, and confidence, the three aspects of the psyche embodied by the Scarecrow, the Tin Woodman, and the Cowardly Lion. Internal tension and turmoil is exacerbated when we become identified with the irritations of daily life and loose touch with these important aspects of ourselves. Dorothy's relationship with each of her companions points to our need to strengthen our sense of self so that we will not become distressed and disconnected when problems arise. Although this healing is essential for our development, to return home we must also bring consciousness into what is hidden and free ourselves from the entrapment of the Wicked Witch and all that she represents.

Homecoming involves being grounded and centered in our sense of self. From this foundation, we can move vertically to encompass the spiritual and metaphysical dimensions of existence. I am reminded here of a tree whose roots burrow deep into the earth, giving it the stability to reach its limbs into the spaciousness of the sky. By establishing a vertical axis from earth to sky, it is able to expand and develop a unique canopy of leaves and foliage. Because they are beyond the physical plane, invisible realms are difficult to describe with words. The leaves of the tree are connected through its branches, just as all beings are connected in the invisible realm of the vertical plane. When the individual concreteness of the horizontal axis and the inter connectedness of being in the vertical axis are experienced simultaneously, these dimensions merge and disappear into a sphere of wholeness and awakening.

It is only with the help of Glinda that Dorothy is able to access and experience the rich multi-dimensionality of her self. In a moment of epiphany when she clicks her heels three times and focuses her intention inwards, the Yellow Brick Road disappears and feelings of separation vanish. In the presence of Glinda, Dorothy's vertical and horizontal axes merge, and she instantly arrives home.

According to Jungian theory, the process of becoming whole involves bridging the conscious and unconscious aspects of ourselves. As a fetus, our physical bodies as well as our psyches are intimately entwined with mother. When we separate from her at birth, our ego develops so that we can function independently in the world. As we grow and develop, the limitations of this ego create feelings of discontentment and unhappiness. We are not the center of the universe, do not have the ultimate power to control our environment, and are unable to fully understand our experiences. The quest for peace and happiness leads us into an exploration of inner experiences, and we begin to explore areas of the psyche that seem quite irrational, confusing, and difficult to understand. Jung calls this unknown and influential aspect of ourselves, the unconscious. He believes we must find a way to explore this dimension of ourselves and bring its content into consciousness to find inner peace and harmony.

For men, it is the development the anima, or feminine, that creates a bridge to unite the conscious and unconscious. As this occurs, a man enters the last stage of wholeness where he constellates the self. Jung believed this is an internal affair that happens in the context of a personal relationship. When he surrenders to a woman and gives up the desire to control life, he opens to aspects of himself that lead towards the final expression of wholeness. For women, the process is a little different. She develops a relationship with her animus, or masculine energy, to access her unconscious and constellate her self. From the experience of wholeness that comes with this union, she sees the fullness of herself as a woman and stands independently as an expression of the feminine. According to Jung, the final stages of the psyche's development for both men and women, involves integrating aspects of the feminine to experience wholeness. In the story of Oz, this happens for Dorothy when she stands before Glinda, the Goddess of the South, and recognizes that she is home.

When I was a teenager, I attended a retreat with a priest who encouraged me to develop my personality. He perceived within me a strong vertical connection with the divine, and suggested creating a foundation for spiritual awareness by understanding the more mundane aspects of the horizontal dimension. As a young adult,

I searched for inner happiness by exploring the psyche and all its levels of functioning. I discovered areas of confusion in my thinking, disturbance in my feelings, and self-doubt and insecurity in my self-concept. Through education, therapy, and personal growth workshops I identified and resolved inner conflicts, developed self-confidence and acceptance, and found that my thinking became clearer and more focused. Although my relationships improved and my life was more successful, I was dismayed to realize that my yearning for inner peace and contentment had not been satisfied. I hungered to return home and like Dorothy, was unaware how to achieve this.

Moments of transformation are profound, undeniable, and often unexpected. Although I had been actively pursuing this path, when the Silver Slippers finally transported me home, my mind was unable to comprehend what had happened. In a desperate attempt to discover the secret of inner happiness, I had abandoned everything that was familiar to me and surrendered into a week of uninterrupted active and silent meditations. Then I joined a large workshop that was attempting to attain inner peace through psychological exploration. In a moment of awakening, all my previous knowledge exploded into prisms of light and color. As if a veil had been torn away, my perception of life was permanently altered. I saw people desperately struggling to change situations that were beyond their control, and frantically fighting to feel good about themselves and their experiences. I also saw the futility of their efforts, and the beautiful perfection of their being that was hidden from their view. I suddenly realized the absurdity of trying to attain what is already possessed. Peals of laughter burst from deep within me as the impact of this awareness permeated my being. The search was over. I was home.

HOMECOMING

Awakening is a strange experience. Everything changes, and nothing changes. Growth and expansion of consciousness continue, the daily stresses of living persist, and the efforts to stay free of past conditioning resume. However, a profound shift in perception permeates all experiences and stimulates a deepening understanding of life. Although we strive for this state as if it is an attainable condition, awareness cannot be possessed or manufactured. It permeates existence and becomes conscious in moments of awakening. Home is opening to life as it unfolds and reveals itself. Through experiencing its fullness each moment, the beauty of divinity manifests as an integral part of daily living. Separation vanishes, and the heart relaxes in love.

The paradox of the journey home is that the final destination actually lies in an unknown place within us. There is no external goal or place to go. Recognition happens in an instant of realization and acceptance. We experience the journey in response to our deepest yearnings, and it acts as a preparation for this unexpected epiphany. It is one of life's strange ironies that we move away from all that is familiar, to discover the object of our search lies within. Although we travel great distances, there is in the end no path that carries us home. Home is the very essence of who we are.

Dorothy's direction is maintained with her desire to return home. Although her path appears confusing at times, it is the clarity of her intention that allows her to complete her adventure. Through her experience in Oz, Dorothy realizes the importance of her family and the richness of her inner life. By facing difficulties and overcoming hardships, she is able to express the potentiality within her.

For me, the experience of home deepened as I wrote this book. I reconnected with family members who were strangers to me as a child, explored the generations from which I emerged, and felt and appreciated the love and support of my immediate family. Old hurts and resentments were replaced with understanding and acceptance as I returned from my own adventures and re-established connections with family and loved ones.

Although I continue to experience a growing contentment with my life, I am most at home when the horizontal plane of my physical existence expands vertically in meditation. My body settles into a quiet position, and I become aware of what is happening within. With external stimulation at a minimum, the intensity of arising thoughts, sensations, and feelings is experienced directly. As this occurs, personal identification with these inner experiences dissolves, and a spaciousness develops that includes all existence. I find myself living from the place of inner peace and contentment I longed to experience as a child. Although disturbances occur, this meditation practice allows me to experience the nature of what is happening with increasing awareness. The roots of suffering unravel as conditioned patterns of reactiveness become more obvious and the bonds of confusion and pain are exposed. Forces of greed, hatred, and delusion dissolve in the ruthless light of consciousness that penetrates most deeply in the silence of meditation. The ringing of bells at the beginning and end of a practice session sometimes reminds me of Dorothy, clicking her heels and surrendering into the experience of home.

INTEGRATION AND RETURN

Living in the world of archetypal energies is thrilling and enchanting. In contrast, the return to ordinary reality can feel mundane, unexciting, and disorienting. The simple routines of daily living dim in comparison with the excitement and extraordinary wonders of altered realities. Although often forgotten, the phase of Return is just as important and stressful as the adventure itself. It is plagued with difficulties and pitfalls, and friends and family frequently find it difficult to relate to the hero or heroine when they return. Just when adventurers need to feel nourished, accepted and loved, they are more likely to be isolated and misunderstood. It takes time for the richness of their experience to integrate into the psyche and be available for others in a form that can be understood. The hero or heroine is frequently left alone to readjust and reorient themselves to a culture that is unable to comprehend the magnitude of what has occurred. At an internal level, they have experienced a transformation that has dissolved old personality patterns and previously held beliefs. Life is experienced with the innocence of a newborn child, and as wondrous as this is, it can also be filled with confusion, self-doubt, and disappointment.

The hero or heroine's journey can take many forms and include many different types of adventure. For some it may be a drug assisted exploration, for others it may come with a near death experience or physical illness. It can appear as a spiritual awakening or battling in a foreign war. Oftentimes seekers become unproductive and lost in seductive fantasy worlds where addictive behaviors predominate. In an attempt to maintain the emotional high and excitement of an expanded state of consciousness, they succumb to the entrapment of self-defeating patterns and relationships. The path of awakening is treacherous, and there are many obstacles to be overcome for transformation to occur. In the last few decades many Vietnam veterans have struggled in this phase without support or understanding. Their experiences have remained unacknowledged and unappreciated by our society in general, and many of them have been unable to resume productive lives as a result. Without the appreciation and receptivity of a loving community, an unrecognized hero wanders alone in a cold and isolated world.

In the Zen tradition, the most profound spiritual adventure is that of enlightenment, or awakening. It is described visually with the Ox-Herding pictures, a series of ten illustrations designed hundreds of years ago to show the pathway of awakening. In the first scene a man leaves his ordinary life and begins looking for the tracks of an Ox. He finds the tracks in the second picture, then finds the Ox, catches the Ox, tames the Ox, and rides the Ox home in the next four scenes. In the next three pictures the Ox is forgotten, the Self is forgotten, and everything merges with the Source from which all things manifest. The last scene is the enlightened one entering the marketplace and coming full circle into ordinary reality. He follows no path, and brings joy, cheerfulness, and an aura of awakening wherever he roams. When the hero returns successfully from his adventure, he resumes the simple tasks of daily living without struggle. Because of his experiences though, he approaches the daily obligations of chopping wood and carrying water from a whole new perspective.

Dorothy returns to Kansas transformed by her experiences in Oz. Although her aunt and uncle are lovingly concerned, they have little understanding or interest in her strange experiences. Their new farmhouse suggests that Dorothy's world has changed totally, but when she first returns, neither Dorothy nor her family realize the depth of this transformation. In later Oz books we see glimpses of Dorothy's new relationship with her family, and watch as she travels back and forth between Oz and Kansas, attempting to assimilate both these dimensions into the wholeness of her self.

Often people come to me now for guidance about integrating their spiritual understanding into the practicalities of daily living. I am reminded of a young man who entered the office after years of following an intense meditation regime. He was confused and upset that he was unable to experience the joy and inner peace that many of his friends were describing as a result of their spiritual commitment. Because the teachings he was following encouraged acceptance of whatever was arising, he suffered silently with a mistaken understanding that he was practicing incorrectly. In therapy he identified a belief within himself that he was not allowed to have what he wanted. He had latched onto the Buddhist teachings of non-attachment to support this position, and could not let himself relax and experience the contentment that arises naturally. Uncovering the source of his discontent brought tears of relief, increased self-acceptance and compassion, and a sharpened discernment of healthy and unhealthy attitudes.

As is true for many spiritual seekers who have embraced the hero or heroine's path, I valiantly resisted this stage of Return. After wholeheartedly embracing a path of spiritual development, I had planned to settle permanently in an ashram in Oregon and thus avoid the strain and stress of integrating into society. However, the skillful perceptiveness of the guru would not support this stance, and I was instructed to return to the world of ordinary reality.

Challenged with the task of remembering and living with a new-found awareness of truth, I was shocked and distressed by the reception I received from close friends and family. As I walked on the beach one afternoon, a girlfriend shared her pain and grief about how I had changed. She was mourning the loss of our relationship, and was not interested in the woman I had become. I was unprepared for the intensity of reactions like these, and longed to return to the protected space of the ashram. I became quite depressed, grieving for the safety, acceptance, and moments of intense insight I had experienced there. Having meticulously followed the spiritual directive to renounce the material world, I was left feeling abandoned and confused. My efforts had seemingly led me into a brick wall. I had simplified my lifestyle by stopping work, dropping personal responsibilities and obligations, and selling my material possessions. When I returned to ordinary reality, I was stripped of my identity, as well as my possessions, and overwhelmed with the simplest of tasks. It seemed I had become weaker instead of stronger, and that my moments of insight were not relevant to the outside world. I was resistant to re-entering the marketplace, and unwilling to consider returning to my previous lifestyle. I kept hoping that somehow the sacrifices I had made would not be in vain. There were few people who understood my dilemma, and I was incapable of articulating the tremendous upheaval that was shaking me to the core.

As I continued to battle the demons of this phase of Return, I slowly began to appreciate the beauty and divinity of simple life experiences. The insights I had attained in the ashram filtered into my daily routines, and I began to incorporate them into my life. The support of spiritual teachers and psychotherapists were invaluable as I reconstructed a life in harmony with my expanded understanding. Old friends emerged, new friendships developed, and I found myself surrounded by a community that appreciated connecting in both horizontal and vertical dimensions.

It has been almost 20 years since I left the ashram and re-entered the world committed to a spiritual path. Now I find people all along this Yellow Brick Road of awakening consciousness. Eager for companionship and reassurance, we provide support and comfort to each other, just as Dorothy and her friends did in Oz. With a sangha or spiritual community, a sense of safety and containment is created that provides a springboard for the journey inwards, and a welcoming committee for the Return. Within its spacious embrace there is room to explore and develop bridges between the richness of the interior world and the demands of the exterior world.

In Western culture, spiritual seekers are on the cutting edge for discovering a lifestyle that supports and cultivates conscious awareness. Buddha addressed this issue with his followers 2,500 years ago, and today we are still struggling to integrate his teachings within a society that has little tolerance for spiritual concerns or practice. My experiences in Osho's ashram showed me how to look behind the screens of illusion and uncover the wizardry of humbugs and well-intentioned balloonists. Although Osho could not take me there, he pointed his finger towards home and provided a place where I could open totally to my unfolding life.

L. Frank Baum wrote fourteen Oz books, and in them Dorothy travels between Kansas and Oz, unable to reconcile her desires to be in both worlds. In *The Emerald City of Oz*, the change in Aunt Em's attitudes are most obvious when she comments to Uncle Henry, "Fairies must have marked Dorothy at her birth, because she wanders into strange places and is always protected by some unseen powers." Uncle Henry is more skeptical, but they both listen to Dorothy's stories eagerly and respect the wisdom she gains through her experiences.

Dorothy's ability to travel between Kansas and Oz shows us how a hero or heroine integrates newfound wisdom. Her reality spans both worlds, and she must learn how to function successfully in each of them. Through this process, she is able to discriminate between healthy and unhealthy situations, and to choose experiences that support her most fully. When her aunt and uncle are forced to foreclose their farm and work in the city, Dorothy is faced with a dilemma. In order to honor herself, she must find a way to preserve her relationship with her family while continuing to expand her associations in Oz. Burdening herself with a lifestyle in the city would prevent her from being able to support her friends in Oz. Although this appears to be a conflict for Dorothy, Princess Ozma of Oz holds a larger vision and quickly responds to Dorothy's distress. Surprisingly, she brings Dorothy's aunt an uncle to the magical kingdom, and provides a farm for them near the Emerald City. Dorothy's energy is now freed to explore uncharted territory and share the lessons of her travels with those she loves. Her inner and outer worlds blend into a rich tapestry of an integrated reality.

At the end of Baum's sixth book, Princess Ozma protects Oz from foreign intruders she fears will ruin the lovely secluded fairy-land. Because "Airships may cause us trouble" she decides to make Oz invisible. Baum hoped to end the series here, but because children clamored for more, he signed a contract with Reilly & Britton to complete an Oz book every remaining year of his life. It seems the fire of Dorothy's expanding consciousness cannot be suppressed, and the collective consciousness of a society awakening insists her adventures be seen. In 1913, Baum resumed contact with Dorothy by means of a wireless radio, and *The Patchwork Girl of Oz* appeared. As his stories intimate, although technological advances can be dangerous, they can also promote communication and creativity.

The Wonderful Wizard of Oz is a story about an interior journey to find peace and happiness. It is a quest that continues throughout our entire lives, and is encouraged by religious teachings around the world. The Bible says "The kingdom of God lies within," and Buddhist passages encourage us to "Look within, thou art the Buddha." Siddha Yoga practitioners remind us that "God dwells within you as you," Hindu followers reveal, "Atman (individual consciousness) and Brahman (universal consciousness) are one." The Islamic faith says "He who knows himself knows his Lord," and Judaism exhorts us to "Hear oh Israel, the Lord our God is one." Recently I saw a refrigerator magnet with Dorothy's picture on it. Its message could be placed in this same category of truths. Carrying the essence of *The Wonderful Wizard of Oz* and repeating the message of masters from around the world it reads, "All you need lies within you."

Oz Is In

CHAPTER ELEVEN
DOROTHY'S INSIGHTS

And oh, Aunt Em, I'm so glad to be at home again.
L. Frank Baum, *The Wonderful Wizard of Oz*, Chapter XXIV

Growing up as Dorothy, I was constantly aware of the legacy of Oz in my own life. I often recreated the Land of Oz in my imagination, envisioning the Yellow Brick Road beneath my feet and hearing the voices of the Scarecrow, the Tin Woodman, and the Cowardly Lion. I walked through my own fantasy world as Dorothy walked through the Land of Oz. I know the feeling of being transported to a world beyond this familiar reality: a world I could access whenever I wanted; a world anyone can access if they believe. Oz is a land of beauty and treasures that reflects the qualities within us all. Oftentimes these gems are left untapped because we don't know how to set them free. The legacy of Oz allowed me to tap into the depths of a world we all yearn to explore. In Oz we can all set these longings free.

Looking back now as Dorothy, I have thought about my journey in Oz and reflected on all the lessons I have learned there. As the Wizard reminded the Scarecrow when he gave him his brains, wisdom comes from our experiences. In order to reap the richness of these experiences though, we need to think about what has happened to us and the lessons we have learned as a result.

Wisdom was the first lesson I learned in Oz, and the Scarecrow was my first friend and teacher. He was self-critical and pained over his lack of brains, but I soon saw that he was very bright even though he had a head full of straw. The more I thought about his problem, the more I realized how important it is to be positive and use your mind to understand and examine what is happening. I saw how much I take my mind for granted. At a simple level, without it we could not remember things or solve problems. We wouldn't know where to find food or how to take care of ourselves. The Scarecrow wanted to trust his judgment and make good decisions, but he didn't think he could. He couldn't really see who he was and had an idea of himself that was quite mistaken. Not only is it important to be able to think, but it is important to recognize the truth, rather than get trapped in our mistaken ideas about this.

The next friend I met in Oz taught me a lesson about love. The Tin Woodman desperately wanted a heart so he could feel love. I began to think about how miserable life would be without love. We would not be able to feel joy or compassion for others, or thankfulness for what we have, or tenderness around a newborn baby. Life would be drab, pointless, and lonely. It seems to me that the heart that makes life worth living. When I feel loved or when I am loving another, I am relaxed, open and happy. The smile on my lips creates bubbles of joy that travel through my body and melt into my heart. The world becomes more colorful and I no longer feel alone. As these feeling deepen, my heart expands and dissolves into everyone I meet.

I've noticed that the heart and head often disagree with one another. One wants to find happiness and the other wants to catalogue, analyze, or figure out what is happening. When I was in Oz, the Tin Woodman and the Scarecrow would often discuss which attribute was most important. The head is good at problem solving and often tries to be in charge. It does not want to listen to the heart though, and often forgets to include the need for emotional connection. Just like the Scarecrow and Tin Woodman, the head and the heart inside each of us must learn to cooperate. Seals and Crofts say "The longest road is from the head to the heart." Maybe this long road is like the Yellow Brick Road. It connects the head to the heart so they can work together.

The Scarecrow and the Tin Woodman did not fight at all while they were with me. They were both willing to follow my lead and help me whenever there were difficulties. Now that I am in Kansas, I feel them both inside me. I usually follow the lead of the heart, because it goes toward harmony and happiness. Then I listen to the head because it helps me handle the difficulties and problems that arise. I appreciate them both, just like I loved the Scarecrow and the Tin Woodman in Oz. When they work together, I feel peaceful and content. The Scarecrow's wisdom gives me understanding, and the Tin Woodman's compassion keeps my heart open and surrounds me with happiness. By listening to both of them I feel peaceful and harmonious, like there is a beacon of light inside to guide me home.

Finally there was the Cowardly Lion who taught me the lesson of courage. He joined us in our quest to find the Wizard because he was scared of the world and trapped behind a mask of bravado. What a hard life he must have had to be King of the Jungle without courage. I can see that if we don't have courage we are afraid to face the truth and then we loose self-respect. We often make things up then so we will look better than we are, and try to intimidate people to make ourselves feel big and strong. It doesn't work though, and like the Lion we end up feeling worse. When the Lion cried in front of me I realized he wasn't happy with his pretense. He was a victim of his own cowardliness. Later in our journey he proved to himself that he wasn't a coward at all. He learned to respect others, and help out even if he was afraid. I watched him gain the respect of everyone he met on our travels, including himself.

All my friends in Oz taught me invaluable lessons. I realized how the mind, the heart, and the courage that lie within need to function together to create a healthy, happy person. Sometimes these aspects push and pull, creating internal conflicts. I've noticed that the mind has all kinds of thoughts. Some make us feel good and some don't. Thoughts come and go, just like feelings. Some feelings make us feel good and others are uncomfortable, but to have none at all is like not being alive. Feelings and thoughts both enrich our lives. I could not function without them, but I can also see that I am different than either one of them. I can see my thoughts and I can feel my heart. Sometimes I wonder who this person is who sees and feels these things. As I ponder this question, words, thoughts, and feelings dissolve into an open sky and disappear.

THE POWER OF GLINDA

Meeting Glinda was the most important part of my journey. When I was with her, I felt happy, wise, and fulfilled. While we talked I could see the brilliance of the Scarecrow, the tender compassion of the Tin Woodman, and the fierce courage of the Cowardly Lion. They already had what they wanted. They always had what they wanted. When Glinda told me how to use the Silver Slippers, I realized home had been inside me all along. I just didn't know it. It really is where my heart is.

With Glinda, I was home in Kansas at the same time I was in Oz. Clicking my heels changed where my body was, but when I saw the new farmhouse I realized that what had happened in Oz was inside of me. Now it is as if I live in both places at once. The things that happen in Kansas remind me of things that happened in Oz. When I get confused or worried I recall how it was in Oz, and then I relax and things get better. If I stay open and follow the Yellow Brick Road, everything works out fine.

I know now there really is no time or space. Everything is contained in this moment, right here and right now. It is all here inside of me. The past is gone, the future has not arrived, and being home is relaxing into this present moment. I don't have to do anything or go anywhere. What is happening here, is also happening there. What was going on then, is also going on now. There are no separations. Outer forms just make things look different.

The mind wants to understand. It likes to separate and divide, so it can study things more carefully and rationally. Without the mind, we have no words. What a strange paradox: when we finally have understanding, there is no way to adequately explain it. Awareness goes beyond the mind, and carries the qualities of wisdom and consciousness.

LEAVING KANSAS

Before I visited the Land of Oz everything in my life seemed gray and lifeless. I knew my aunt and uncle loved me, but I didn't feel happy inside. My mother and father had just died, and my aunt didn't know how to take care of me the way I needed her to. I was scared and lonely, and I missed my parents. When the cyclone came and blew me off to Oz, everything changed. I had landed in a world of color and beauty. It was like a fairy godmother waved a wand that transformed my world forever.

When I got back to Kansas, everything looked different. Before Oz, I didn't think magic existed. When I got back I knew that it did. It made everything sparkle and shine like the glistening gems in the Emerald City. Even the gray flatlands of Kansas were more colorful when I got home. It's funny how everything seemed to have changed, even though it really stayed just the same.

I once made a postcard that said "To believe in yourself is magical." I've though about that often since I returned from Oz. My time there made me feel strong inside and more aware of all positive things that happen around me. Now I see my cup half full, instead of half empty. When I wake up every morning I remember I can choose how to look at this cup, and when I see it in a positive way, I feel more content. Even when things are difficult, I can feel the presence of the Good Witch of the North. I remember how her lips kissed my forehead, and feel protected by her once again. Sometimes I still feel surrounded by invisible forces that tickle my imagination and disrupt my expectations. When I try to hold onto these experiences they dissolve and disappear. When I open my heart and allow awareness to expand, these magical moments multiply.

Life changed so much when I got back from Oz. I hardly ever feel bored or unhappy like I did before the cyclone carried me away. I feel stronger, wiser, more loving, and more courageous. It's like the Scarecrow, the Tin Woodman, and the Cowardly Lion live inside me now, and I can remember the lessons of our adventures anytime I want.

THE WIZARD'S CHALLENGE

I was quite lost when I arrived in Oz, but I had felt lost in Kansas ever since my parents died. I was so relieved when the Wizard said he could help me. I believed in him totally, and was devastated when he turned out to be a humbug. Since my visit to Oz I've learned that no one can give us what we already have, even if we don't know we have it. I've also learned that everything we need is inside. We're all the same, and like children we playfully discover the truths we have forgotten.

I surprised myself when the Wicked Witch of the West tried to take my Silver Slippers. I didn't want to fight her, but became enraged when she tripped me. I had walked all over Oz in those Silver Slippers. They made me feel strong and free and independent. She had no right to take them from me. I felt bad that I hurt her, but I also felt good about standing up for myself and defending what was mine. I don't like to fight, but I discovered that sometimes we have to protect ourselves. Before I met the Wicked Witch I felt like such a little girl. I was unable to make the simplest decisions for myself. Being in Oz forced me to grow up though. After melting the Wicked Witch, I became much clearer and more sure of myself.

When I was young I was taught not to talk to strangers. When I arrived in Oz everyone was strange, and I had to decide what to do. I quickly recognized who was safe and who was not, and had to forget all the rules I

had been taught. Now that I am back in Kansas this is still true. People try to tell me how things are and what I should do, but most of the time their information confuses me. If I pay attention to what I'm feeling inside, life seems to flow easily and smoothly. Sometimes I get scared though, and doubt myself. Then life's river gets rocky and difficult to navigate.

I've noticed this river of life is most disturbed when I want something. My feelings become more intense and I often find myself angry, disappointed, or upset. When I don't expect things though, I am more open to what is available and everything I need comes my way. The Wizard taught me a lot about this, even though he disappointed me terribly. He really was a kind man, but he wasn't all-powerful like I wanted him to be. I know a lot of people who pretend to be something they are not. I used to get so confused when their promises disappeared like the Wizard's hot air balloon. I understand now, people hide behind masks that misrepresent who they really are. I see through these facades more easily though, and am more relaxed and loving as a result.

THE POWER OF LOVE

Being with the Scarecrow, the Tin Woodman, and the Cowardly Lion was a real blessing while I was in Oz. Although we were very different, we loved and respected each other tremendously. I like to be with other people, but sometimes I get so caught up in what they need that I forget where I'm going. In Oz it was different though. I was so determined to get home that even my companions couldn't distract me. I loved being with them, and they helped me a lot. We took care of each other and we all got what we wanted. This was a new experience for me. I realize now that everyone is traveling on the Yellow Brick Road of life, and that helping each other is an important part of the journey.

Although it was difficult to be with Aunt Em and Uncle Henry after my parents died, when I was in Oz I wanted to go back to them. I knew they'd be worried about me. Even though they had a lot of problems, I knew they loved me. I couldn't imagine living without them. But after I was in Oz for a while, the Scarecrow, the Tin Woodman, and the Cowardly Lion became another family for me. Now I have a family on the outside and one on the inside. I used to hope that someday we could all live together in one place. Now I realize that we do all live together, and my home encompasses both Kansas and Oz. I can travel between them whenever I want, and they both live inside me all the time.

One of the things that surprised me most in Oz was that all the animals and characters talked. I liked that because I could ask them questions and talk about things that upset me. When the Cowardly

Lion attacked Toto I was angry, and jumped up to swat him on the nose. I was shocked when he burst into tears, but when we talked about what was wrong I could see how scared and insecure he was. He didn't know how to handle himself, and our conversation helped. Having him on the journey was important for all of us.

When I'm scared or angry or confused, I usually blurt out what is upsetting me. Then those feelings melt away like the Wicked Witch, and I begin to talk about what is disturbing me underneath. If I don't talk about these things, they grow into big monsters, and trap me in their dungeons of darkness. I know now I have to free myself from those dark places. Often I call on the courage of the Cowardly Lion to help me. Later I feel lighter and happier, and can travel more freely like I did with the Wicked Witch's magic cap.

WISDOM AND COMPASSION

Visiting Oz has allowed me to develop the things I value most in life: wisdom, compassion, and courage. Wisdom comes from experiencing life's richness as it reveals itself. Compassion comes as the heart opens and lovingly recognizes the oneness of all beings. Courage comes from recognizing the truth, responding to life's challenges with compassion, and acting with authenticity. The Scarecrow, the Tin Woodman, and the Cowardly Lion gave me valuable insights into each of these. It's surprising how they couldn't see what they already had. The Scarecrow wished he had a brain, but didn't realize that he was already very smart and wise. The Tin Woodman wished for a heart, but didn't realize he was already very compassionate and loving. The Cowardly Lion wished for courage, but didn't realize that he was already very brave. Oftentimes we don't know ourselves until a situation arises where we respond spontaneously and then realize who we are by the way we behave. The Scarecrow was able to understand problems and figure out ways to solve them. The Tin Woodman loved all creatures and was outraged when he saw injustice. The Cowardly Lion acted boldly and confidently when he was helping his friends.

From my adventures in Oz, I learned that you can do anything you want to do as long as you take care of yourself and don't hurt anyone. Although sometimes we have to fight to protect ourselves, most of the time we can solve problems by talking about them. The most important things you want in life are already within you. Loving family and friends are gifts to be treasured. Accepting yourself and your circumstances brings boundless joy and happiness. Opening fully to life's experiences allows you to soar freely in the skies of creation. Allowing yourself to be open to the possibilities of traveling beyond this reality and accessing experiences from the realms of the imagination may be one of the most powerful gifts we can give to ourselves.

Chapter Twelve

The Baum Legacy Lives On

Life was a serious thing to Dorothy, and a wonderful thing too, for she had encountered more strange adventures in her short life than many other girls her age.
     L. Frank Baum, *The Emerald City of Oz*, Chapter III

Sparkling rays of sunshine slid through stormy clouds illuminating a vast expanse of open land. Before me stretched a long valley and in the distance, rolling hills extended into the rugged mountains of eastern Oregon. All signs of civilization dropped away as I entered into the territory of the spiritual master. Although I had stopped using my given name of Dorothy many months before, my mind kept creating images of the Oz heroine arriving at the Emerald City, eager for an audience with the Wizard. I hoped that he would tell me how to live so that I could experience a peace and happiness that would never end. It seemed I had been traveling on the Yellow Brick Road through many lifetimes, and finally had reached my destination. Brilliant patterns of light danced onto the rich velvet surface of Mother Earth, creating a magical welcome into the strange and unknown territory. With eyes opened wide in anticipation of the fulfillment of my heart's desires, I carefully maneuvered my van around the last curves of the dusty dirt road and descended into the valley below. I had left behind all that was familiar in my life and entered the ashram of the Indian mystic Osho Rajneesh. It was a strange paradox. Separating from my family allowed me to see more clearly my relationship to Dorothy and *The Wonderful Wizard of Oz*. I felt as though I was living the story of

Dorothy now, or perhaps the story was living through me. It was as if the phenomenon of Oz expanded beyond the pages of L. Frank Baum's book weaving into the fabric of life itself.

I grew up in middle class America, one of many baby boomers born after World War II who grew into a flower child as I passed into young adulthood. At that time, *The Wonderful Wizard of Oz* was a familiar fairy tale that addressed the perils of feeling like a small child lost in a strange and unfamiliar country. The story was simple and easy to understand, and the images in the movie captivated the imagination of the little girl inside me who boldly adopted the façade of a rebellious adolescent. My generation was acutely aware of the problems inherent in our society and eager to eliminate all sources of injustice, inequality, and suffering. As we entered adulthood, we fought with the enthusiasm of children to create a new order where harmony and understanding predominated.

Since early childhood I had been searching for something that would satisfy the confusion and longing in my heart. Even as a young child my mother told me I was trying to understand the purpose of life. Just as Dorothy was determined to return home, I yearned to discover inner peace and happiness. I knew this involved my relationship with God, and actively explored the world of spirit in hopes of attaining this precious state.

With the reasoning of Dorothy I imagined I needed a Wizard to magically grant my heart's desire. I assumed that if I worked hard and was a good girl I would eventually find this powerful man who could fulfill my wishes. I was a romantic who believed a Wizard might come in the form of Prince Charming. He would love me unconditionally and eagerly carry me into a land of happily ever after. I was relentless in my pursuit of happiness, and willing to explore in whatever way required. Discovering how to be free of suffering became a personal as well as a professional goal. I knew that healing the emotional pain of others required the resolution of my own internal struggles. I began therapy, joined encounter groups, experienced a plethora of consciousness raising workshops, and attended numerous professional conferences.

Although in childhood I had resisted the controls and expectations my family placed upon me, as a young adult I followed a path I hoped would bring recognition and approval. My father was a physician, my mother a nurse, and I worked hard to please each of them. I was married four years before my first son was born. I continued working, and developed a successful practice as a psychotherapist before the birth of my second son, a few years later. The stress of raising two boys, establishing a career, and attending to the struggles in my marriage was all-consuming. There was no time for inner reflection as I fought to maintain an image of perfect wife, mother, and therapist. My younger son was just three years old when the marriage dissolved. My father died after a brief illness that same year. Everything I had built over the last twelve years seemed to crumble, and I began to search with renewed vigor for the happiness I dreamed of as a child.

THE HEROIC FEMININE

The marriage of L. Frank Baum and Maud Gage introduced the fiery, independent energy of my great-great-grandmother, Matilda Joslyn Gage, into the family. She was the descendant of a Revolutionary War veteran, and adamant in her pursuit of liberty. When U. S. citizens were forbidden to aid runaway slaves in 1850, she signed a petition refusing to obey that law. She harbored escaped slaves through the Underground Railroad, and worked for their emancipation as a member of the Loyal Women's National League. Through this group she made contact with the woman's suffragist movement and devoted herself to the cause of universal suffrage. The inscription she had placed on her tombstone speaks for itself. "There is a word sweeter than mother, home or heaven. That word is liberty."

I was named Dorothy after my mother's mother, Dorothy Hilda Duce, who married Frank and Maud's youngest son, Kenneth. Although neither the Baums nor the Duces approved of the match, Dorothy entered the Baum family and the legacy of the Oz heroine appeared in concrete form. It is as if L. Frank's imagination conjured the image of Dorothy, and she became manifest in physical form as my grandmother. Years after my grandmother died, I came along to continue the passage of Dorothy through the family lineage.

My own call to freedom has rocked my soul for as long as I can remember. I felt restricted as a child and eager to cast aside the chains that encumbered me. Although I was raised with few rules or external constraints, I felt the stifling limitation of my parent's conservative attitudes and beliefs. Like many of my generation, I insisted on experiencing life free from the veils of other's expectations, and rebelled by defending the inherent right to follow my own inner guidance. Although I began with the enthusiasm and innocence of a child's vision, my life long quest has been to free the spirit and heal the internal pains that have passed through generations.

For many years, living in close association with the fictional image of Dorothy created confusion about my personal identity. Just like her, I needed to separate from my family in order to discover who I was. When my father died suddenly the same year that my husband and I divorced, I felt like a cyclone had ravaged through my life. I fought frantically to establish a sense of meaning and order in the chaos that was surrounding me, and clung to the disciplines of yoga and meditation as islands of sanity and safety. From this tenuous position I began to address the spiritual yearning within my heart.

LETTING GO

I remember the day I stood gazing through the familiar security of my living room windows and decided to explore another way of living. I willingly left the comforts of home to pursue a life free of my conditioned upbringing. My husband had left the previous year and I had established myself as a single mother. I was terrified that my life would become a series of repeated failures, and knew I had to explore unknown dimensions to break the unconscious patterns that dominated my experiences. I had been living by the rules and attempting to create happiness by doing what I was told. Although I had created material success and outward stability, my inner world had been neglected and ignored. Now it was time to follow my ancestors and step outside the confines of other people's expectations.

I was drawn to the Indian mystic Osho Rajneesh, and intrigued with his integration of western psychology with eastern mysticism. After attending a four-day retreat at the beginning of 1982, I longed for the bliss I saw on the faces of his sannyasins, and quickly embraced this path. In India, a synnyasin is a spiritual seeker who renounces the material world and lives without personal possessions. Determined to honor my inner spirit without compromise, I sold my possessions and moved to Osho's ranch in Oregon. I thought this Indian guru was the Wizard who would help me find the way home.

The first challenge I faced at the beginning of this Yellow Brick Road was receiving a spiritual name and dropping my identity as Dorothy. Cold fingers of fear traveled down my spine and gripped my belly as I separated myself from the familiar support of family and friends. In one brief moment of surrender I became Ma Dhyan Anugita which means "music that follows meditation." The name seemed to lift a burden of responsibility from my shoulders and I wondered at how quickly things shifted after that.

Followers of Osho wore orange and red clothing in those days, just as sannyasins in India wear ochre robes. Daily decisions about dressing were reduced to a simple selection from shades of pink and red. Somehow this little change freed me from feeling obligated to please other people. Although I prided myself on being independent, I had compromised myself in many ways to conform to the expectations of others. I was relieved and delighted with the sense of spaciousness that began to surround me. Old ideas and outdated perceptions crumbled, and veils of illusion dropped away to reveal the truth of what was hidden within me.

I spent a wonderful few months in the Emerald City of Rajneeshpurim before I was told through Osho's secretary to go live wherever I wanted and be happy. Although I accepted this situation as the unfolding of my path, just like Dorothy I was shocked and dismayed by the Wizard's message to me. The first phase of my journey in Oz was complete, and now I was required to leave the safety of the Wizard's castle and confront the Wicked Witch of my internal fears and self-doubts.

It is only in retrospect that I can appreciate the role my children played through these tumultuous years. They provided me with focus and stability as I soared into the world of spirit. Dorothy's determination to return home was fueled by her love for her family. In the same way, Brian and Greg forced me to stay connected with the physical plane while my spirit expanded into invisible realms.

Because women value their relationships with others so highly, we struggle to relate in the outside world while maintaining close associations with loved ones. This struggle is the main focus of Dorothy's journey in Oz. She had to leave the safety of home to grow and expand, but was determined to maintain a connection with her family and return to her roots. Her journey in Oz is an example of how to establish independence and develop individuality, while valuing and honoring personal relationships.

When I look at the story of Dorothy, I understand the strong intuitive need to stay connected with family while establishing a separate identity. When I was eighteen I eagerly left home to attend college, but returned every summer to share and discuss new insights. My thoughts were not always appreciated, but the urge to communicate was strong. I hoped my parents would acknowledge and support who I was becoming. Although I was often disappointed with their response, severing our relationship felt self-violating. I wanted to find a way to include them in my world while maintaining my independence. As I have continued to relate with my family, I have been challenged to stand up for myself and find my voice as an adult. Staying connected with them, as Dorothy did, has encouraged me to expand and develop in ways beyond my expectations.

Although it has been difficult, understanding my roots has been a provocative and intense stimulus for understanding myself and my adult relationships.

DOROTHY LIVES ON

I feel honored and humbled to be the personal embodiment of Dorothy, the young heroine who is beloved by so many. I experience her energy in a focused and personal way, somehow manifesting her archetype in the collective, while maintaining my identity as an individual. I am aware that this embodiment is both impermanent and illusory. Who I am is beyond the spoken word and outside the realm of conceptual thought. Although my parents named me Dorothy, I call myself Gita to remember my essential nature. Ultimately, I believe it is the spiritual task of each one of us to become conscious of the manifestation of spirit in concrete form. From studying this fairy tale I see that my spirit lives through the archetypal energy of Dorothy. Participating in this living legacy creates a bridge between the worlds of invisible phenomena and physical reality.

As the popularity of *The Wonderful Wizard of Oz* increases over the years, I feel I am being catapulted forward by a giant tidal wave beyond my control. The relevance of this image in my life manifested strongly in a dream I had many years ago. Terror griped my heart. Before me advanced a tremendous wall of water. I noticed the immensity of this wave when it was barely visible on the horizon, and as it approached the shore, it became a growing mountain of water. I stood transfixed, unable to divert my eyes form the moving edifice. There was no escape. My throat was so dry I could barely swallow. White sand lengthened before me as the wall of water sucked the shoreline into its undulating mass. I was trapped. There was no place of safety. In the next moment however, I was moving towards a mosaic of leafy green trees and weathered rooftops. I was traveling with the wave, at a tremendous speed over the land. My eyes gazed in wonder at distant snow-covered mountains, while my feet struggled for balance on a thin surfboard that separated me from the horrifying depths below. I awakened from the dream still striving to stabilize myself on this moving mountain of water.

Over the years I have learned to enjoy surfing the ever-changing waves of life. Sometimes the seas are calm and placid, while at other times they are wild and stormy. I let go of trying to control the forces of nature by focusing on the position of my feet. When properly secured on the surfboard of awareness, I flow with the water's movement and marvel at the mystery of existence and the richness of my experience.

CHAPTER THIRTEEN

CREATING YOUR OWN YELLOW BRICKS

My greatest wish now is to get back to Kansas.
L. Frank Baum, *The Wonderful Wizard of Oz,* XXIII

Avalanches of psycho-spiritual books, tapes, and workshops flood the market, promising blissful states of consciousness and prosperity. We are satiated with enlightened masters and charismatic teachers from around the world who make themselves available through the media to encourage self-improvement, spiritual development, and life style enhancement. For the seeker of truth, it is challenging to discern what is most nourishing for the soul. Like creating a road of yellow bricks in a strange and Oz-like world, we must find and develop our own wisdom and compassion amid this plethora of enticing promises and well-intentioned teachings.

The Wisdom of Oz is not another self-help book, personal growth regime, or attempt to solve life's difficulties. It is written to encourage Oz lovers to explore their own path of yellow bricks. Baum's fairy tale is about looking within to discover what is already there. I suggest you take time for personal reflection to see what messages Oz holds for you.

The following questions and suggestions are designed to stimulate your ideas about the story. They arise from the experiences and feedback of Oz workshop participants. Some of you may want to examine this material by talking with friends, while others may want to develop ideas through writing. You may find artistic media more expressive for your feelings. I encourage you to explore in a variety of different ways so you can easily access the wisdom that resides within you. Through working with these questions, you may become more aware of the wisdom, compassion, and courage you already possess. Reflecting on the pattern of life's journey helps to reinforce direction and re-establish a sense of purpose and meaning. Sharing insights with others creates a sense of community that is tremendously reassuring and supportive.

You might find it helpful to keep your thoughts in a journal or notebook. They can then become a springboard for further reflection and meaningful conversation. You might find it stimulating to read a chapter of *The Wisdom of Oz* out loud with a friend, and let discussions or creative projects develop from what has been read. Those of you who are therapists, teachers, and counselors may find these questions and suggestions useful to generate group projects and discussions focusing on self-reflection.

As you know from the story, friends are valued companions for finding the way home. What is most important though, is awakening the expression of your own inner wisdom so that you can realize the beauty of home in your own heart. The following suggestions are offered to assist you on this path. Please feel free to create your own ideas or projects, as you get more involved with the Oz story.

QUESTIONS ABOUT THE JOURNEY

What do you imagine happens in a place over the rainbow?
If you were going on a journey to an unknown place and could take
only one small bag. What would you put in it?

If you were traveling with a group, what strengths and resources
would you want in your fellow travelers?
How would your presence benefit the group?
How would your group decide where to go and what to do?

How do you typically handle difficulties and obstacles?

How and when would you return home?

Make up a story about your journey.

> Describe where you are going, and what you experience as you reach your destination.

> What does this story show you about yourself and your attitude towards life?

QUESTIOINS ABOUT THE SCARECROW

Who in your life reminds you of the Scarecrow? Why?

How are you like the Scarecrow?

What helps you think clearly?

Imagine and write about a situation where you solve a difficult problem.

> What happens next in your story?

QUESTIONS ABOUT THE TIN WOODMAN

Who in your life reminds you of the Tin Woodman? Why?

How are you like the tin Woodman?

How do you reconnect with your heart when you feel trapped in an armor of self-protection?

Imagine and describe a situation where you opened your heart without reservation. What happens next in your story?

QUESTIONS ABOUT THE COWARDLY LION

Who in your life reminds you of the Cowardly Lion? Why?

How are you like the Cowardly Lion?

When you act defensively, what are you feeling inside?

Imagine and write about what would happen if you behaved more authentically in a particular situation. Describe what happens next.

QUESTIONS ABOUT THE WIZARD
Who in your life reminds you of the Wizard? Why?
How are you like the Wizard?

What would you ask from a Wizard?
What would be required to obtain your request?

How do you hope to be rescued in your life?
How do you react to disappointment?

QUESTIONS ABOUT THE WICKED WITCH
Who in you life reminds you of the Wicked Witch? Why?
How are you like the Wicked Witch?
How would you describe your dark side or shadow?
How does the Wicked Witch hold you captive?
How can you escape from her?

When is anger justified?
How do you react when someone wants something that is yours?

Create a story where you want something and are asked to perform
    a difficult task to receive it.
    Describe the situation you are in and explain what led up to it
        and what happens next.

QUESTIONS ABOUT YOURSLEF
What Oz character do you identify with most?
How are you like that character?

How would you describe home?
Where are you now in your journey home?

After a transformative experience, how does it feel to reconnect
    with friends and family?

Describe situations where you have stepped out of the innocent attitude of childhood and activated the power of your inner resources?

How has instinctual energy served you in your life?
Describe a situation where acting instinctively was destructive for you
Describe a situation where it was positive.

ARTISTIC WAYS TO EXPLORE OZ

Draw a picture of your favorite scene in the story.
Write about what you drew and why you drew it.

Write your own Oz story:
Make up your own characters.
Include situations that remind you of your own life.
Let the characters find creative solutions for their problems.

Draw pictures on yellow construction paper of ways you feel about different parts of the story. Lay them down like Yellow Bricks to tell a story about your life.

Draw or paint a Yellow Brick Road on big sheets of butcher paper and include:
the tornado,
the Emerald City,
the Wicked Witch's castle,
Glinda's castle,
the surrounding countryside,
the obstacles on the journey.

Add other parts of the story that are important to you.

Make a picture, collage, or clay representation of:
> Each of the characters.
> A scene from the story that you react to strongly.

Write about your drawing, painting, collage, or clay project.
What do you see when you look at it?
How did you feel when you were working on it?

MOST IMPORTANTLY.

Have fun with these suggestions!!
And feel free to create more of your own.

For Your Information

OZ BOOKS BY L. FRANK BAUM IN CHRONOLOGICAL ORDER

The Wonderful Wizard of Oz. Chicago: George M. Hill Co., 1900.

The Marvelous Land of Oz. Chicago: Reilly & Britton Co., 1904

Ozma of Oz. Chicago: Reilly & Britton Co., 1907

Dorothy and the Wizard in Oz. Chicago: Reilly & Britton Co., 1908.

The Road to Oz. Chicago: Reilly & Britton Co., 1909.

The Emerald City of Oz. Chicago: Reilly & Britton Co., 1910.

The Patchwork Girl of Oz. Chicago: Reilly & Britton Co., 1913.

Tik-Tok of Oz. Chicago: Reilly & Britton Co., 1914.

The Scarecrow of Oz. Chicago: Reilly & Britton Co., 1915.

Rinkitink in Oz. Chicago: Reilly & Britton Co., 1916.

The Lost Princess of Oz. Chicago: Reilly & Britton Co., 1917.

The Tin Woodman of Oz. Chicago: Reilly & Britton Co., 1918.

The Magic of Oz. Chicago: Reilly & Britton Co., 1919.

Glinda of Oz. Chicago: Reilly & Britton Co., 1920.

FOR MORE INFORMATION ABOUT OZ

The International Wizard of Oz Club

www.ozclub.org

FOR MORE INFORMATION ABOUT SANDPLAY
Sandplay Therapists of America
www.sandplay.org

DR. GITA MORENA
Is available for private consultations, Sandplay training and seminars, presentations, and retreats. Check out her website at www. gitamorena.com or dorothygitalive.com

BAUM FAMILY TREE

Benjamin Ward Baum (1821-1887) and Cynthia Ann Stanton gave birth to L. Frank Baum in 1856. He was the seventh of nine children.

Matilda Joslyn (1826-1898) and Henry Hill Gage (1818-1884) gave birth to Maud Gage in 1861. She was the youngest of five children.

L. Frank Baum (1856-1919) and Maud Gage (1861-1953) married in 1882 and gave birth to 4 boys

Frank Joslyn Baum (1883-1958) married Helen Snow in 1906 and gave birth to Joslyn Stanton and Frank Alden.

Robert Stanton Baum 1886-1958) married Edna Ducker in 1914 and gave birth to Robert Allison, Stanton Gage, and Florence Ducker.

Harry Neal Baum (1889-1967) married Mary Niles in 1910 and gave birth to Harry Neal and Judith Gage. Later he married Brenda Holter in 1942 and adopted her children, Richard and Anne Holter.

Kenneth Gage Baum (1891-1953) married Dorothy Hilda Duce (1892-1945) in 1914 and gave birth to two daughters.

Janet Hilda Baum (1922-2004)

Ozma Frances Baum (1916-1999) married Kenneth Austin Mantele (1914-1981) in 1945 and gave birth to a daughter and a son.

Dorothy Anne (Gita) Mantele (1947-) married David Joseph Morena in 1969 and gave birth to two sons

Brian Guiseppe (1973-)
Gregory David (1977-)

Craig Fredrick Mantele (1949-) married Mimi Dowling in 1973 and gave birth to Megan and Austin.

FAMILY PHOTO ALBUM

Matilda Joslyn Gage (c. 1860)
The character of Dorothy embodies the strength and determination
Baum must have seen in his mother in law, Matilda Joslyn Gage.

L. Frank Baum in a topcoat on his wedding day, 1892.

Maud and L. Frank Baum had four boys. From top left they
are Frank Jr., Harry and Rob. Gita Dorothy's grandfather,
Kenneth, is seated in front between his parents.

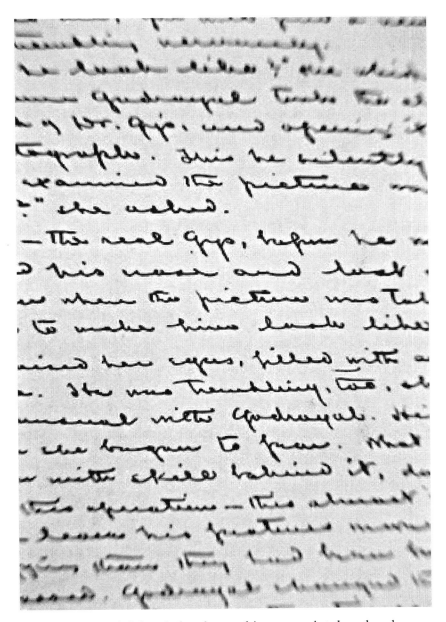

Baum was left handed and wrote his manuscripts long hand
Before typing his final copy. Here is a page from *Aunt
Jane's Nieces in the Red Cross*, published in 1915.

In 1910 the Baum's moved to Hollywood and named their home Ozcott. The wallpaper in the bedroom was changed frequently because Baum would wake in the middle of the night and scribble his thoughts on nearby walls. (c.1940)

The garden at Ozcott. Baum usually wrote in the afternoons, edited his material the next morning, and tended the garden for relaxation and pleasure. (c1915)

One of Baum's favorite pastimes was tending flowers. They were
of showcase quality and he had many trophies for his hobby. One
of his strains of chrysanthemums he named Matilda (c1915).

Baum with the directors of the Oz Film manufacturing Company
in 1914, Louis Gottschalk, Clarence Rundel and Harry Holdeman.
The group was founded in 1913 and produced numerous
silent films before it was sold to Universal Studios in 1916.

Baum was a member of the Los Angeles Athletic Club and founded a club within the club, which he called "The Lofty and Exalted Order of Uplifters." Baum is pictured here, dancing with dramatic flare (c.1914)

Family picnics were a favorite activity of the Baums. Here L. Frank and Maud are seated with their grandchildren. Their granddaughter Ozma is on the right in the arms of her grandfather, L. Frank. Dorothy and Kenneth, Ozma's parents, stand behind Maud on the left. (c. 1918)

Maud with Oz book. After l. Frank died, Maud carried on the legacy.
She was present at the opening of MGM's *The Wizard of Oz* movie
in 1939, and lived at Ozcott until her death in 1953. (c.1940).

Maud and her four sons, Frank, Kenneth, Harry and Robert (c. 1903)

Years later, the earlier photos of Maud and her
four sons was replicated (c. 1948)

L. Frank's youngest son, Kenneth, was an adventurous young man who enjoyed all sorts of outdoor activities. (c1912)

Auto motoring was one of Kenneth's favorite pastimes. (c. 1910)

Dorothy Hilda Duce married L. Frank's youngest son Kenneth
at Ozcott in 1914. She died in 1945, two years before her
granddaughter Dorothy (Gita) was born. (c. 1914)

Ozma and her cousin Robert were close in age and visited
Ozcott frequently as young children. Here L. Frank Baum holds
them together in front of his Hollywood home. (c.1918)

L Frank insisted that his first granddaughter be called Ozma.
Here she wears the locket engraved with her name that
he gave her a few weeks after she was born. (1919)

Kenneth and his wife Dorothy had two daughters,
Ozma (right) and Janet (left), shown here in 1985.

Dorothy (Gita) is pictured here with her mother, Ozma, and
grandfather, Kenneth, L. Frank's youngest son. (1947)

The Baum women were proud descendants of Matilda Joslyn Gage.
Here Maud stands in the middle with daughter-in-law Dorothy
on her left and Granddaughter Ozma in front of her. (1920)

Ozma was an RN when she met Kenneth Mantele, a doctor
in the hospital where she worked. They were married while
he was on leave from his military service in 1945.

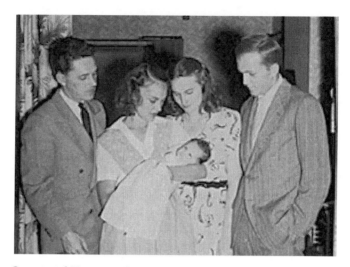

Ozma and Ken gave birth to Dorothy Anne (Gita) in 1947.
She was christened in the Episcopal Church in the presence of
her parents and her Aunt Janet and Uncle John (1947)

Dorothy (Gita) shown here as a curious toddler ready to explore
the world as her mother, Ozma, keeps a watchful eye. (1948)

Craig was born to Ozma and Ken in 1950. He married Mimi Doering in 1977 and they have two children, Megan and Austin. (1997)

Ozma returned to school when she was 70 years old to fulfill a life-long dream of obtaining a masters degree in Human Behavior. (1991)

Gita's children, Brian and Greg, grew up surrounded with the
Oz imagery that inundates our culture. Here the Cowardly Lion
and Tin Woodman pose for a picture with them. (1980)

Brian (left) works in the field of cinematography as a camera man
and operator. It seems he shares his great great grandfather's
interest in film and photography. Greg (right) is an entrepreneur
and owns a growing business consulting firm. (1998)

Cynthia Tassini, L. Frank Baum's niece (Harry Baum's daughter), stands here between Dorothy (Gita) and Ozma. (1994)

Ozma's 80th birthday was a grand family reunion at the Coronado Hotel in San Diego where L Frank and Maud enjoyed vacationing in the early 1900's. (1996)

Dear Oz Lover,
Just like Dorothy we are traveling in a strange land.
Along the way we do our best
to make friends, face dangers, venture into the unknown
and discover our heart's deepest desires.

Dorothy shows us the way.
She stays open, moves forward, helps her friends,
and stands up for who she is.

May you be inspired by her journey and enjoy
wondrous moments of light, love and laughter.

Dr. Dorothy

GITA DOROTHY MORENA
www.dorothygitalive.com   www.gitamorena.com

Psychotherapist Jungian Sandplay Consultant Seminar Leader Author
Great Granddaughter of L. Frank Baum, author of The Wonderful Wizard of Oz
Licensed Marriage, Family & Child Therapist

Made in the USA
Columbia, SC
08 January 2024

30107224R00126